The Hamlyn Guide to
Football
Collectables

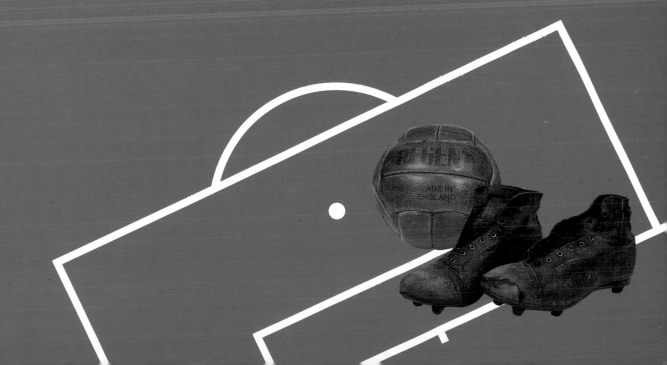

The Hamlyn Guide to
Football
Collectables

Duncan Chilcott

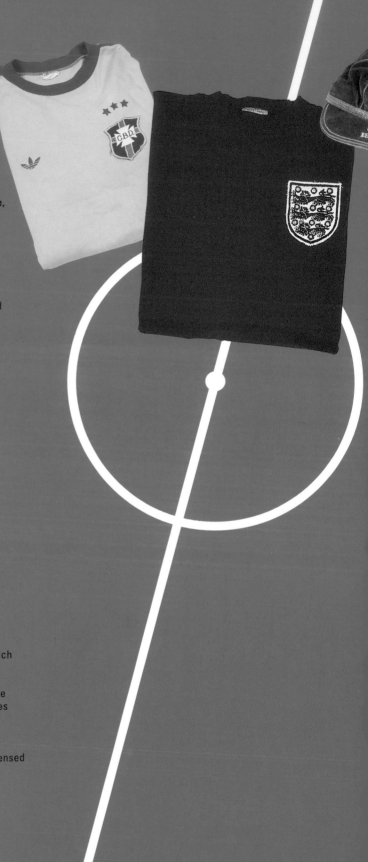

**This book is dedicated to football enthusiasts every-
where and to Lizzie, my wife, without whose patience,
inspiration (and permission), this book would never
have been written.**

Hamlyn Football Collectables
Duncan Chilcott

First published in Great Britain in 1995
by Hamlyn an imprint of Reed Consumer Books Limited
Michelin House, 81 Fulham Road, London SW3 6RB
and Auckland, Melbourne, Singapore and Toronto

Executive Editor Alison Starling
Project Editor Katie Piper
Text Editor Peter Arnold
Executive Art Editor Vivienne Brar
Designers Emma Jones, Geoff Fennell
Production Heather O'Connell
Index Richard Bird
Special Photography Ian Booth, Fiona MacSporran

ISBN 0 600 58819 X

A catalogue record for this book is available from the
British Library

Set in A Garamond, Franklin Gothic and Univers Condensed
Origination by Scantrans Pte Ltd, Singapore
Produced by Mandarin Offset
Printed in Hong Kong

Matt. Busby

Contents

Introduction

Compared with the collecting of items connected with golf and cricket, the organized collecting of football memorabilia has, until recently, been relatively low key. This is surprising if one considers that football is generally considered to be one of Britain's national sports. Since as recently as the late 1980s however, football memorabilia has slowly but surely grown in popularity. This has led to auction houses presenting sporting sales that either contain sections of football memorabilia, or are solely devoted to the game. Dealers in sporting items have also begun to seek out football memorabilia with greater enthusiasm as the hobby has expanded. The growth of these auctions and dealers has been reasonably slow and many people who remember collecting in the early days, speak wistfully of the bargains to be had in the 1960s and 1970s.

Today established collectors, or those wishing to begin collecting football memorabilia are spoilt for choice. There are many collecting clubs and associations, magazines and directories, specialist auctions and dealers in most parts of the country whose job/interest it is to help and advise football collectors. In addition to these collecting clubs, publications and services, are the well-stocked supporters shops at most football clubs, where collectors can purchase contemporary "collectables". Such shops provide most collectors with the ideal starting point for any collection; indeed most seasoned collectors keep their eyes as much on football souvenirs of the 1990s as they do on collecting football memorabilia of earlier years. Today's soccer souvenir is tomorrow's collectable football memorabilia, be it a school-boy size Manchester United FC second-choice away strip from their 1993-94 double-winning season, or a team portrait poster of Tiverton Town, from the Great Mills League, beaten 1-0 by Bridlington Town in the 1992-93 FA Challenge Vase final at Wembley Stadium.

The hardest decision a collector is likely to have to make is what to collect. This is, however, rarely a conscious choice because collections and collecting preferences tend to evolve over many years as different interests develop. Most collections begin with one or two football match programmes or a school boy football autograph book. If the hobby then begins to grow to grow, these will soon be added to with more of the same or by some other collectable aspect of the game. And because so much football memorabilia is ephemeral, it is generally quite affordable. Old match programmes, autographs, postcards, cigarette cards, tickets, stamps, books and publications, contemporary examples of which remain popular and are mostly generally available, can usually be purchased for a few pounds and are all recognized areas of collecting, having their own clubs, auctions and publications.

Ephemera does not interest all collectors of soccer memorabilia; some are more interested in "living" memorabilia, such as football jerseys, medals and awards, caps and football equipment, such as old football boots, items that have been worn by, awarded to, or owned by footballers throughout the history of the game. This type of collecting interest has an immediacy that is easy to understand; after all, which football fan would not want to possess Geoff Hurst's England international shirt from the 1966 World Cup final; Billy Wright's 100th England international cap; Tommy Gemmell's European Cup winner's medal or Eric Cantona's football boots. These, and similar items, have a universal popularity which make them irresistible to football collectors everywhere. A collector may wait many years for such a piece to appear for sale.

This book aims to guide the collector through the huge and diverse selection of football collectables on the market, whilst giving advice on the relative importance of condition and quality, giving where possible a price guide. The values given in this book reflect the sort of prices you might expect to pay for similar pieces at an auction house or a dealer. As there are so many variable factors involved in the pricing of antiques and collectables, values should be used as a general guide only. It also aims to place collectables in the historical context of a player, team, season, country, or football in general and to guide collectors around some of the pitfalls waiting to deceive them, such as reproductions. I hope this book will pass on some of the enthusiasm fellow collectors and I have for the subject, and inspire you in your search for new and exciting items.

DUNCAN CHILCOTT

Duncan Chilcott is Managing Director of the auction house, Bonhams West Country, and has specialized in sporting memorabilia for over ten years. He is the author of the Which? Guide to Collectables, *has appeared regularly on the* Antiques Roadshow *for the past six years, and runs an antiques advice line for BBC Radio Devon and BBC Radio Bristol.*

Programmes

To many football fans, who loyally and regularly turn out to support their team in all weathers, the humble football match programme is an important and integral part of their enjoyment of the game, as best material for pre-match, half-time and post-match entertainment. While, collectively, programmes can form an interesting season-on-season encyclopedia of facts and information, charting the highs and lows of football clubs, the football programme also serves as an important part of a club's public image and a useful mouthpiece for both manager and chairman, as well as a souvenir of the match *and* a collector's item.

Some early 20th century programmes were published with newspaper-type titles such as Aston Villa's *The Villa News and Record*, Fulham's *The Cottagers Journal* and *The Chelsea F.C. Chronicle*. Within the pages of these and other old programmes lies a fascinating insight into football of yesteryear: pictures and information on the players, teams and characters;

match reports; soccer-related stories, news and opinions of the day; together with a liberal sprinkling of period advertisements for football kit and equipment. They also promoted non-football products (including cigarettes!), endorsed by the football idols of the day. Programmes can also give a flavour of the social and political history of the period – for example, wartime programmes that feature air raid warnings.

Today, match programmes are the most popular area of football collecting by far. It is likely that football programmes have been collected since the earliest days of organized football during the latter part of the 19th century, when programmes were little more than team sheets or single page advertising bills. Very few of these early examples have survived; however, as the forerunners to today's big glossy programmes, they are important and collectable.

Over the past 25 years the programme collecting hobby has developed considerably, becoming a well-organized pastime with guide books and specialist periodicals published to aid and inform collectors, together with programme fairs, dealers and auctions to visit. Large sections of auctions of football memorabilia are devoted to programmes. Single, rare programmes may fetch large sums of money, but there are usually lots of multiple programmes on offer, which enable the collector to build a collection quickly and relatively inexpensively. Going to auction views, usually held during the week before a sale, is a good way to increase your knowledge and familiarity with football programmes in particular, and football collectables in general.

Football programme collecting clubs also abound, often associated with football clubs and supporters' clubs, where like-minded enthusiasts meet and share their interest with each other. (Addresses for some collectors' clubs and associations are featured at the back of this book.)

Fortunately, in this popular field, the collector is faced with a wide choice of collecting categories. Many choose the programmes of their favourite team, while others specialize in international matches or club competitions and collect the programmes from World Cup and European Championship tournaments, or domestic and European cup competitions. In recent years, non-League football programmes have become increasingly popular with collectors. Here, the choice and variety is wider than ever as the smaller minor-league clubs are beginning to realize the commercial potential of publishing match day programmes.

Left: A rare Aston Villa programme for their German tour in 1938. *Background image:* A programme for the 1938-39 FA Cup second round replay between Walthamstow Avenue and Stockport County. *Above:* A USA '94 World Cup official programme for the final between Brazil and Italy in Los Angeles on 17 July 1994.

League Club Programmes1

When collecting or investing in football programmes it is worth remembering that, as with most other antiques and collectors items, the condition of collectable programmes is very important. Many collectors will only collect programmes that are in good condition and will not consider examples that are defective or damaged in any way. Adopting such high standards can make collecting awkward and expensive; however it is always a good idea to collect the best examples available – taking both price and rarity into consideration. Most of the football programmes illustrated or featured in this section are pre-1950, and while it is possible to maintain a modern collection of programmes in a perfect state, it is more difficult to achieve the same with examples that may be up to 90 years old! So it is vitally important that collectors know how to look after their programmes and that they are not tempted to pay over-the-odds for poor examples or "lemons".

◀ Brentford FC was founded in 1889. These three programmes were issued between 1930 and 1939: (left) Brentford v Notts County (Div. 3), 1930; (centre) Brentford v Aston Villa (Div. 1), 1935; (right) Brentford v QPR, 1939.

£20-40 each

▼ Two programmes produced by Portsmouth FC (est. 1898) featuring FA Cup fifth round matches in 1931-32 and 1938-39: (left) Portsmouth v Arsenal, 13 February 1932. Portsmouth had a good FA Cup run during this season, but lost 2-0 to Arsenal; (right) Portsmouth v West Ham United, 11 February 1939. Portsmouth defeated the Hammers 2-0, before progressing to a Wembley Stadium final, where they caused a major upset by the FA Cup for the first time, beating Wolves 4-1.

£40-70 each

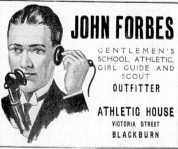

◀ This useful programme issued for Blackburn Rovers v Arsenal on 15 October 1932, was No 4 of a new series issued by Blackburn during the 1932-33 season. Arsenal beat Blackburn 3-2 in this match and went on to win the League Championship. Arsenal scored 118 goals during the season and Blackburn conceded 102, both the highest for the division.

£60-80

▼ This FA Cup fourth round replay between Aston Villa (est. 1874) and Portsmouth on 27 January 1932, ended in a 1-0 defeat for Villa. Aston Villa was one of the founder members of the Football League in 1888, and the club's first programme was issued in 1906. More recently, good examples of that programme have sold for as much as £1,000.

£40-60

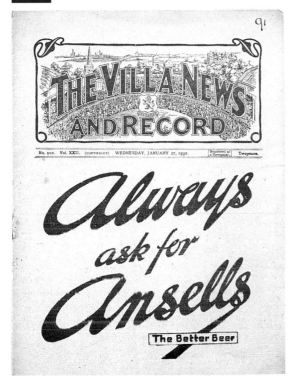

▲ These three programmes were produced by Arsenal FC (est. 1886) between 1930 and 1939. From left to right: 1929-30 season, League Division 1, Arsenal v Everton, 8 February 1930; Arsenal v Portsmouth, League Division 1, 27 August 1938; Wartime League, South "A" match, 2 December 1939, Arsenal v West Ham United. This last example is a simple team-sheet programme with an air raid warning at the bottom of the page.

£20-40 each

▼ Three Clapton Orient (est. 1881) programmes from Division 3 (South) local Derby matches between 1933 and 1939: (left) Clapton Orient were beaten 3-1 by Charlton Athletic on 2 December 1933; (centre) Clapton Orient v Crystal Palace, 20 October 1934, marked five unbeaten games in a row for Orient; (right) Orient drew with QPR on 15 April 1939, at the end of a poor season.

£60-80 each

► These three programmes featuring Brighton and Hove Albion FC (est. 1900), including two examples from 1932-33 (against Chelsea and West Ham) and another from 1939-40 (against Fulham) show a range of cover designs from the 1930s.

£60-80 each

◄ Two 1930s programmes issued by Luton Town: (left) an FA Cup third round match against Arsenal, 13 January 1934, containing a tribute to recently deceased Arsenal manager Herbert Chapman; (right) Luton Town v Sheffield Wednesday, 26 August 1939.

£40-60

League Club Programmes 2

Programmes were not originally designed ever to be as highly valued and keenly collected as they have become today. Most were simply purchased to be read on match day, and were then thrown away shortly afterwards. Consequently, many older programmes, which have survived to become collectable today, are damaged in some way or another. Tears and creases, stains and dirt, pen or pencil markings, damp and fading are the usual defects commonly found on programmes, and can reduce their desirability and value. Do not attempt to mend tears with sticky tape: ordinary adhesive tapes often turn a dark colour and peel off over time, leaving unsightly marks. Non-staining tape is available. Most multi-page programmes are bound using simple steel staples. These often rust if kept in damp conditions and can mark the paper. The staples can be carefully removed, and the programme can then be stored in a clear plastic wallet to ensure that it does not fall apart.

▼ This well produced programme for Watford v Queen's Park Rangers, 30 January 1932, includes two full pages of club gossip in which the editor, slightly surprised, announces: "We now have the honour of including in our list of Vice-Presidents, a lady!"

£40-60

▲ Southend were enjoying a successful season in 1931-32, and were second in the Third Division prior to this game against QPR on 16 April 1932 – which resulted in a 0-0 draw.

£40-60

◄ Shown here are three match day programmes issued by Crystal Palace FC between 1933 and 1938, for matches against Norwich City (FA Cup first round), Cardiff City (Div. 3) and Walsall (Div. 3). These are smart, compact, 12-page publications, that include amusing football cartoons borrowed from *Punch* together with caricatures of players by A. J. M. entitled "Palace Sportraits".

£30-50 each

▶ Ipswich Town's issues from the 1930s, such as this one, Ipswich Town v Aston Villa, 11 January 1939, are among the best pre-war programmes, with 24 high quality pages of pictures, gossip and competitions.

£30-50

▼ Two programmes produced for West Bromwich Albion (founded 1879). The 12-page programme, left, from a Division 1 match against Arsenal in January 1932, is full of interesting gossip and information, but has few illustrations. The 1945 programme, right, is shorter (eight pages), and was produced for an England v Wales "Victory International", the first of this group of matches to be played on English soil. A near-capacity crowd of 56,000 saw Wales win 1-0 through a goal by Aubrey Powell of Leeds United.

£30-50 each

▲ The Wolverhampton Wanderers ground at Molineux has played host to FA Cup semi-finals. The programme on the left is from the Everton v West Ham semi-final in 1933, won 2-1 by Everton who went on to win the Cup. The programme on the right is from an FA Cup sixth round match between Wolves and Everton on 4 March 1939. This is a good quality programme which includes a picture of the Molineux Grounds in 1871.

£50-80 each

◀ A compact and useful programme from an FA Cup game between Leicester City and Arsenal during the 1934-35 season, this piece is in good condition except for some writing on the cover, and a pair of rusty staples.

£20-40

League Club Programmes 3

Collecting programmes is one of those hobbies that can quickly mushroom and, without care, collections can build up without form or continuity. Therefore it is advisable for collectors to plan their collectionsand avoid simply going out and amassing anything and everything of interest. Choose the category or type of programmes that are to be collected, and before allowing the collection to get too large, decide on storage, finance and even insurance. Remember, an uncatalogued and uninsured collection, stacked in cardboard boxes and stored in a garden-shed, will rapidly become a poor and valueless collection. When starting a collection many people begin by collecting programmes of their favourite team. Other favourite areas of specialization are internationals and other big matches, such as FA Cup finals or European games, and programmes of non-League and ex-League clubs. However, it will soon become apparent to programme collectors that the choice of categories is endless! Inevitably, the scope of the collection broadens and other areas of interest become catered for.

► A 16-page compact match programme published by Sheffield United during the 1907-08 season, this example is in a partly disintegrated condition. Due to acidity the pages are turning a dirty-brown colour and have become brittle.

£50-80

◄ Three typical 1930s Tottenham Hotspur programmes from between 1933 and 1935, with covers decorated with topical cartoons by Jos Walker. The programme on the left is from March 1933, in the season the team was promoted to Division 1. In the centre is an example from February 1934, also a good year for Spurs. But in 1935, right, they were relegated to Division 2 once again.

£20-40 each

► Bolton Wanderers issued this programme for a Division 2 match against West Ham in April 1935. Relatively uncommon, look out for pre-war Bolton programmes as they are often interesting pieces.

£50-70

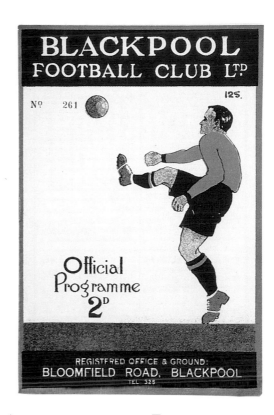

▲ This issue of *The Reading FC Record* for Reading v Millwall, January 1933, is a single, large printed sheet, folded in four, which has the feel of a newspaper and needs to be unfolded in a similar way. This FA Cup third round replay was the third meeting of these two clubs in the competition following one game that was abandoned after 70 minutes due to fog, and one match that was drawn. Millwall won this match 2-0.

£30-50

▲ In contrast to some of the grander programmes issued by wealthy clubs in high divisions, this simple four-page example was produced by Gillingham FC and contains only basic information, with no club gossip or editorial comment. Playing recently relegated Millwall in a Division 3 (South) match during the 1934-35 season, Gillingham were expecting tough opposition, and sure enough Millwall won 3-1.

£20-40

▲ In extremely good condition, this programme was issued by Blackpool FC for an England v Ireland Home International game held in Blackpool in October 1932.

£250-300

▼ Arsenal programmes for games against Manchester United in February 1958, the last United League game before the air disaster, and from 1959.

£40-60 for the pair

◀ These three examples of Queen's Park Rangers programmes, issued between 1932 and 1934, illustrate how often a club's programme designs could change. In these seasons the club was languishing deep in Division 3 (South).

£30-50 each

Ex-League Club Programmes

Today, when we watch or read about the Manchester Uniteds, Liverpools and Arsenals of the world of Association Football, it is easy to forget the many clubs in the lower divisions that struggle from week to week to make ends meet. But since the formation of the Football League in 1888, over 30 clubs have left it for one reason or another. Some resigned, usually for financial reasons, others were dismissed because they failed to be re-elected and had their places taken by more successful non-League clubs, while a few did not apply for re-election and simply disappeared. Together with the clubs featured on these two pages, the list of former League clubs includes names such as Aberdare Athletic (1921-27), Bootle (1892-93), Durham City (1921-28), Glossop North End (1899-1915), Merthyr Town (1920-30), Thames (1930-32), and Wigan Borough (1921-31). Programmes from football matches featuring ex-League clubs, both home and away fixtures, are very sought after by collectors for their rarity value and soccer history interest.

◄ Founded in 1921 in Wallasey, New Brighton joined the League for the 1923-24 season, but because of its proximity to the Merseyside clubs, the team found there was not enough support to go around, and left after the 1950-51 season.

£80-100

◄ When this programme was published during the 1928-29 season, Bradford Park Avenue was enjoying some success in Division 2 having been promoted from Division 3 (North) as Champions the previous season. During the 1930s the side was one of the strongest in Division 2, but their fortunes declined after 1950s and the team finally disappeared from the League in 1970.

£50-80

► Aldershot FC was a member of the Football League 1932-92. Many famous players guested for the team during World War 2 when many army units were based in the town. Aldershot won this match against Millwall in 1937 2-1.

£30-50

◄ Southport FC was founded in 1881 and became Southport Central and Southport Vulcan, before reverting to Southport in 1919. The club applied for re-election to the League eleven times, before the application finally failed in 1978.

£30-50

◄ Accrington Stanley is not the Accrington club which helped to form the Football League. Stanley joined the League in 1921 and resigned during the 1961-62 season. This programme is for a 1946-47 game played at Peel Park.

£40-60

▼ Third Lanark FC, one of the original eight clubs that formed the Scottish FA in 1873, went into liquidation in 1967. The side which began life as the team of the Third Lanarkshire Rifle Volunteers, achieved great success in the late 19th and early 20th century, winning the Scottish FA Cup (1889 and 1905) and the Scottish League in 1904. This programme is for a match in 1946-47 against Queen of the South, which ended in a 1-1 draw.

£40-60

▲ Barrow Association Football Club was formed in 1901 and turned professional in 1908. The team joined the League in 1921 as an original member of Division 3 (North), but was expelled from the League in 1972. Today it is a member of the Northern Premier League. This programme is typical of those published by Barrow AFC during the 1938-39 season.

£30-50

▲ Gateshead AFC was founded in 1899 as South Shields Adelaide and elected to Division 2 as South Shields in 1919. The club was relegated in 1928 and two years later moved to Gateshead and changed its name to Gateshead AFC. The club failed to gain re-election to the League in 1960. This programme, dated 16 April 1955, was produced for a match against Accrington Stanley (see above).

£40-60

Wartime Football Programmes

When Neville Chamberlain formally declared war on 3 September 1939, it was immediately recognized that football could make a significant contribution to the war effort. It was widely accepted that the game had a beneficial effect on the nation's morale and fitness. By October competitive League football had been re-organized into eight regional leagues in England and two in Scotland. Players contracts were suspended so they could "guest" for any club they chose – though that normally meant the clubs nearest to where most troops were stationed, such as Aldershot. The FA used its experience and organization to arrange football at all levels. The better players were in constant demand and still managed to play a great deal of football. Sadly, not all footballers were so lucky and 75 professionals lost their lives during the war. Paper was rationed throughout the conflict and as a result football programmes were usually short, poor quality publications, and were frequently innacurate due to last minute changes.

▲ This Army International between the Army in Scotland and the Army in England in aid of Army Charities, was played on 28 October 1944.

£10-15

▲ Programmes for friendly matches such as this, Metropolitan Police Professionals v Football Association XI, played on 3 April 1941, are quite rare because the games failed to attract the large crowds that Football League games or internationals did. This example is in fair condition.

£20-40

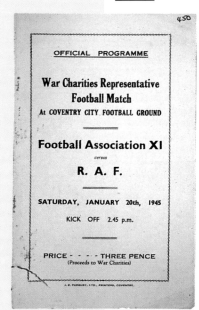

◄ This War Charities Representative Match between the FA and the RAF on 20 January 1945, was played to benefit the Red Cross and St John Fund and the RAF Benevolent Fund. The 12,750 spectators had the rare opportunity of witnessing some truly great players lined up against one another. The FA side included Len Shackleton, Tommy Lawton and Joe Mercer, while the RAF team featured Stan Mortensen and Stanley Matthews. The RAF defeated the Football Association team 6-4, which included a hat-trick from Mortensen.

£10-15

▲ Red Cross Charity matches became an important part of the wartime football scene. Between November 1939 and March 1940 there were eleven such matches. The FA v The Royal Air Force matches were already a regular fixture prior to the war, the FA having won 12, lost one and drawn two of the series. In this game on 30 March 1940, a strong RAF side beat the FA XI 3-2.

£20-30

▼ This Inter-Allied Services friendly match between the Metropolitan Police Professionals and the Royal Air Force, held on 4 June 1941, was their last game of the 1940-41 season and had the added attraction of being played at Wembley Stadium, loaned free of all charge for the occasion. The crowd of 10,000 spectators was treated to an entertaining contest which the RAF won 6-3. Both teams included players of quality, with the Police featuring the skills of Leslie Compton (Arsenal), for example.

£20-30

◄ A double-bill fixture staged at Stamford Bridge on 2 June 1941 of which the Inter-Allied Services Cup Final between the Army and the RAF was the main attraction. During the war both sides were able to call upon an impressive amount of football talent to represent them including many international and future international players, such as Swift, Hagan and Scott. The Army defeated the RAF 8-2.

£5-15

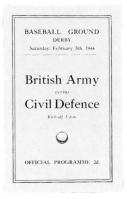

▲ The programme from this British Army v Civil Defence match on 5 February 1944 indicates the number of stars playing for these teams. Certainly Derby County supporters would have enjoyed watching their skipper, Jack Nicholas, playing for the Civil Defence, with two pre-war Derby players, Jimmy Hagan and Ronnie Dix, appearing for the British Army.

£15-30

◄ This game, RA Depot (Woolwich) v A London Representative XI, played on 12 May 1945 a week after VE day, was arranged by the London clubs to thank the Depot players for their help on numerous occasions during the previous seasons of wartime football. The Representative XI was a strong side with a number of international players, and although widely expected to be the first team to defeat the Depot in two seasons, they lost 3-2.

£10-15

21

FA Cup Programmes 1

Eight years after the formation of the Football Association, a committee met in July 1871 to institute the Football Association Challenge Cup. The idea was later ratified in October of the same year and a small silver trophy costing £20 was purchased for the competition. This original FA Cup, which became affectionately known as the "Little Tin Idol", was eventually stolen while on exhibition at Birmingham, after being won by Aston Villa in 1895. There were 15 entries for the opening competition of the Challenge Cup (as it was then called), and the final was played on 16 March 1872 at the Kennington Oval between The Wanderers and the Royal Engineers. The crowd of 2,000 spectators not only witnessed The Wanderers win 1-0, but also the first final of a competition that soon ranked in popularity with the Derby and Grand National. It is unlikely that a programme was ever issued for the first Cup finals, or at least not in the form that collectors would recognize today – simple team sheets were possibly produced, but frustratingly none are known to survive.

◀ This 75-year-old programme from the FA Cup final (Spurs v Wolves), 23 April 1921, is in particularly poor condition. It has been folded into quarters causing many pages to tear and the spine is severely distressed. In spite of this damage, it is rare and very collectable.

£400-600

▲ Newcastle United beat Arsenal 2-1 in the final held on 23 April 1932, a match renowned for a disputed goal. This piece, featuring articles by Charles Buchan, is in good condition with no serious tears or creases.

£200-300

▲ The 1925 Cup final between Sheffield United and Cardiff City was held on 25 April. Although this programme appears to be in poor condition, dirty and torn, with writing on the cover and a damaged spine, it has never been folded, and the cover has not been "repaired" with sticky-tape, and the pages within are in good clean condition. Sheffield won the game 1-0.

£300-400

► The programme for the 1927 FA Cup Final, Arsenal v Cardiff City, held on 23 April, features an advert for Players' Cigarettes that includes a cutting from the *Liverpool Evening Express* which claims "Cup-Tie Players' Cigarettes – Trainers do not object – They know what is good for them."! In this match Cardiff wrested the FA Cup from an English team for the first and only time since 1872.

£250-300

▼ The 1934 final, Portsmouth v Manchester City, was an exciting game, eventually won by Manchester City 2-1. City's right half-back was Matt Busby. This programme is a complimentary copy, that has unfortunately been folded in half leaving a sharp crease across the whole programme.

£150-200

▲ The centre-spread plan of the field of play in this programme from the April 1936 Cup final, Arsenal v Sheffield United, appears above a typical advert from the period: "A player may Miss Kick but he mustn't Mrs Bovril."

£150-200

▲ The 29 April 1933 "all-Lancashire" Cup final between Everton and Manchester City was interesting because it was the first in which the players were numbered, to help the 93,258 spectators and news-reel commentators identify them. Everton achieved a 3-0 victory, and completed a remarkable treble, with their Division 2 Championship in 1931, and their League Championship in 1932. This programme is in reasonably good condition apart from minor wear and tear, and staples that are beginning to rust.

£150-200

FA Cup Programmes 2

FA Cup programmes probably appeared during the later years of Queen Victoria's reign, and a copy is certainly known to exist for the 1886 final played at Kennington Oval on 3 April between West Bromwich Albion and Blackburn Rovers. This early programme was little more than a single page team sheet, giving details of players' names and positions, the umpires and the referee – Major Marindin, RE (President of the Football Association). The result was a 0-0 draw. The two teams replayed at Derby County on 10 April where Blackburn Rovers won by two goals – thereby recording the last ever hat-trick of FA Cup wins, 1884, 1885 and 1886. In 1923, Bolton Wanderers defeated West Ham United 2-0 in the first ever Wembley FA Cup final, but unfortunately it was probably the most unsatisfactory match ever decided in the history of the competition. While 126,047 people passed through the turnstiles, a further 100,000 managed to rush the barriers. The police had to clear the pitch of spectators to allow the game to take place, and throughout the match the crowd encroached on the pitch, often interfering with play! The programme for this final is now one of the most prized possessions amongst collectors; an original copy in good condition is becoming increasingly rare. However, collectors should be aware that exact reproductions do exist.

◀ Newcastle United won the 1952 FA Cup final against Arsenal on 3 May 1952, becaming the first club to win the Cup in successive seasons since Blackburn Rovers in 1891. Apart from some writing, this piece is in good condition.

£30-50

▲ Tottenham Hotspur's first FA Cup final appearance at Wembley was on 6 May 1961 (above left), and in that year won the double. They also won the Cup in 1962 (above right).

£20-40 each

◀ Arsenal beat Liverpool 2-0 in the 1950 FA Cup final. It was Denis Compton's second last game for Arsenal, and he insisted on being revived with brandy at half-time. Reg Lewis scored both goals. This programme features statistics, articles and pictures.

£20-40

▲ This autographed programme is from the first FA Cup final after the war, on 27 April 1946, between Charlton Athletic and Derby County.

£150-300

▶ An official programme from the FA Cup final between Huddersfield Town and Preston North End that took place on 30 April 1938, this piece has obviously been folded in half and thrust into a pocket in the past, leaving a crease running across the centre. The two metal staples have rusted, leaving brown stains, and the pages are unbound, which reduces value. This was the first Wembley Cup final to be decided by a penalty, scored by George Mutch.

£80-120

▼ Princess Elizabeth presented the FA Cup to Wolverhampton Wanderers following their 3-1 defeat of Leicester City in the 1949 Cup final on 30 April. According to the programme Don Revie, who later managed Leeds United and England, was due to play for Leicester City, but he was forced by injury, to listen to his team lose over the radio from a Leicester infirmary bed.

£30-60

▼ The programmes issued for the 1939 Cup final, held on 29 April, between Portsmouth and Wolverhampton Wanderers also include the "News Chronicle Community Singing song-sheet". Although this example has been folded, the presence of the song-sheet is a definite bonus. Portsmouth were the surprise winners of this, the last Cup final before the war.

£100-150

▲ The 1958 final between Bolton Wanderers and Manchester United on 3 May took place just three months after the Munich disaster. Matt Busby's hastily rebuilt side, consisting of four Munich survivors together with new signings, was beaten 2-0 by a strong Bolton side.

£20-40

Inter-League Programmes

The first Inter-League game was played in defiance of the FA on 11 April 1892 at Bolton, between the Football League and the Scottish League. The result was a 2-2 draw before a crowd of 9,500 spectators. The original object of the Inter-League games was to provide revenue for the discharge of the work of the League; however they soon became an invaluable aid in the building of the English, Scottish and Irish national teams. They also gave football clubs in the smaller cities and towns in Britain, such as Preston and Plymouth, an opportunity to stage representative matches. The first match to feature the Irish League took place in Belfast in 1894, where England won 4-2, while Eire had to wait until the 1946-47 season for their first Inter-League representative match. By the 1950s the Inter-League games were beginning to lose their popularity – they had never attracted the spectator support enjoyed by full international matches. The Football League eventually abandoned Inter-League competitions in 1976. Inter-League match programmes make an interesting and alternative collecting category.

◄ This 12-page programme was issued for the English-Scottish League match on 2 November 1938, the 44th of the pre-War series, and the first ever to be played at the modernized Molineux ground, Wolverhampton.

£40-60

◄ An official programme for the Scottish League v English League match, held on 23 March 1949, their 46th peacetime meeting. The English League continued a winning streak, and won this game 3-0 with goals from Jacky Milburn (Newcastle United), Tom Finney (Preston North End) and Stanley Mortensen (Blackpool). This eight-page programme features a typically dramatic cover in the distinctive Scottish style.

£30-50

► Preston North End FC had the honour of being selected to stage this English-Irish League match at their Deepdale ground on 14 April 1948, where the Football League defeated the League of Ireland again, this time by 4-0.

£20-40

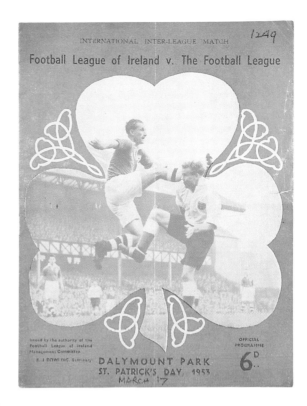

▲ This attractive and unusually stylish pro-gramme, published by the *Ulster Sports Gazette* on behalf of the Irish Football League for the 41st match of the Irish League-English League series, held on 22 October 1947.

£20 40

▲ It is clear from the pages of this large, attractive pro-gramme for the Eire-England Inter-League game of 4 April 1951, that the Irish were looking foward to, but not expecting to win, this game. In the event they lost by a single goal.

£20-40

▲ This 16-page illustrated programme was produced in Ireland for a game played on St Patrick's Day 1953, that resulted in a 2-0 defeat for the home side.

£10-20

▼ For this Scottish-English Inter League game played on 25 March 1953, the Scottish team included the talents of Lawrie Riley, Sam Cox and Bobby Evans.

£30-50

◀ This programme from the Irish League v English League match on 23 September 1953 features portraits of the team captains Johnny Matthews (Glenavon), and Billy Wright (Wolves), on the front cover.

£10-20

England International Programmes 1

The first official international took place between Scotland and England on Saturday 30 November, appropriately St Andrew's day, 1872 at the West of Scotland Cricket Club in Partick. A healthy crowd of 4,000 spectators turned up to watch, each paying one shilling. The English had intended to give the Scottish a lesson in the game – however the Scots team contained the English and the game ended in a draw. Simple team sheets may have been printed, but there is no evidence that a programme was produced for the occasion. Tickets were issued for the match and existing examples are believed to be the oldest tickets for an international football match. Possibly the oldest existing football programme is a team sheet for a friendly played at Hampden Park on 9 March 1875, between Queen's Park (Scotland) and Wanderers (England). An interesting feature explained by this programme was that as players did not wear numbers on their shirts, they were identified by the colour of their stockings or caps! For example, C. Herriot (Queen's Park) wore a black and white cap and no stockings, while Hubert Heron (Wanderers) sported grey stockings and an orange, violet and black cap.

► This piece from England v Scotland, 31 March 1928, is in "fair" condition because, although uncreased and untorn, it is dirty and the staples have rusted, staining the paper. Scotland's "Wembley Wizards" won 5-1.

£100-150

◄ On 21 October 1953, an historic fixture was held between England and "The Rest of the World", as a celebration of English football. The 20-page official programme cost the spectators one shilling. The England side included stars such as Billy Wright and Stanley Matthews, and a last-minute penalty by Alf Ramsey earned England a 4-4 draw.

£40-60

► This simple 20-page programme from 5 April 1930 was produced for a Home International contest between England and Scotland. On this occasion, under the captaincy of Arsenal's David Jack, England beat a formidable Scottish side 5-2.

£80-120

▲ The Home International match between England and Scotland on 14 April 1934, was the fifth on the Wembley pitch and the 58th of the series. The state of this programme is typical: most importantly it is complete, and is in overall good, but not mint, condition.

£100-150

▼ This friendly match between England and Argentina on 9 May was one of many events staged for the Festival of Britain in 1951. Argentina had not appeared at Wembley before and her players were regarded as great soccer artistes, but England won 2-1.

£30-40

▼ Unfortunately this 20-page programme has been folded in half at some time, and all the pages bear some creases, which will reduce its value – probably by 50 per cent or more! It was produced for a notable game featuring some great players, the FA Centenary Match (1863-1963), England v The Rest of the World (FIFA) held at Wembley on 23 October 1963.

£30-40

▼ On 9 April 1932, England defeated Scotland 3-0 at Wembley in a match to decide the 1931-32 Home International Championship. This programme, a complimentary copy, contains pictures, fact and articles by Charles Buchan – the former England and Arsenal player, and member of the *News Chronicle* sports staff.

£80-120

► A well-illustrated piece, this programme is of an England v Belgium match held on 26 November 1952. The Belgian team had an English coach – ex-Blackburn Rovers and Northampton Town goalkeeper, William Gormlie, who is profiled in this programme. Successful so far during this season, beating the skilful Italian side 2-0, and the Dutch 2-1, the Belgian team was defeated 5-0 by an England side featuring Alf Ramsey, Billy Wright, Nat Lofthouse and Tom Finney.

£30-40

England International Programmes 2

In January 1922 building work began on "a great national sports ground" in the pleasant and rural suburb of Wembley, six miles from the West End of London. It took only 300 working days to complete and was christened the Empire Stadium. It cost £800,000 to build, was 890ft (271m) long, 650ft (198m) wide and 76ft (23m) high, and used 2,000 tons of steel and 25,000 tons of concrete. The first International match to be played at Wembley was between England and Scotland on 12 April 1924. The programme published for this occasion was a large, colourful and well-illustrated publication, with 28 glossy pages. But it cost one shilling, which was very expensive at the time, and today examples are rare and highly prized. Prior to the construction of the Empire Stadium, many football clubs and sports grounds in England had hosted the nation's international games, but after the early 1950s most England international home matches were played at Wembley. Programmes for non-Wembley internationals are usually rarer than those for games played at the Empire Stadium, but tend to be less sought-after by collectors.

◀ This programme was issued for England v Yugoslavia, on 22 November 1950, where a Highbury crowd of 61,454 saw Yugoslavia draw 2-2 against an England side that included Leslie Compton and Nat Lofthouse.

£20-40

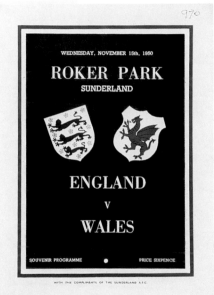

◀ The England v Wales match at Roker Park, Sunderland, 15 November 1950, was only the third international to be staged at the ground during its 53-year history (both earlier games were against Ireland, in 1899 when England won 13-2, and 1921). This programme, a complimentary copy, is quite rare. England's domination over the Welsh continued with a 4-2 victory in this match.

£30-50

▶ The performance of the England football team in the immediate post-war period contained no hint of the shocks to come, with victories over Northern Ireland, Eire, Wales, and Holland, and a 1-1 draw in this match with Scotland on 3 May 1947.

£30-40

▲ England won this Home International Championship/World Cup qualifying match (see above right) against Ireland 3-1, on 11 November 1953.

£20-40

▲ This highly informative programme from England v Italy at White Hart Lane on 30 November 1949, is in good condition except for minor stains from rusting staples.

£20-40

► An article by Ivan Sharpe in this programme from England v Ireland in 1949, explains that the four British Football Associations had rejoined FIFA in 1946, and the 1949-50 Home International Championship had become a qualifying group for the World Cup finals to be held in Brazil in 1950.

£20-40

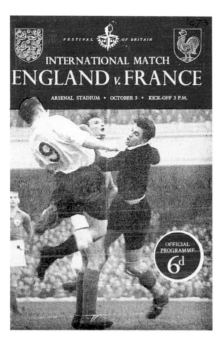

▲ As their contribution to the 1951 Festival of Britain the FA arranged a "Festival of Football" including six international matches and a number of games between British and Continental clubs. England's full international team remained unbeaten in their three Festival of Britain games, played against Argentina, Portugal and France. This piece, issued for England v France, 3 October 1951, has been folded in half and has been written in, though otherwise it is in reasonable condition and also complete.

£20-40

▼ A rare piece, this programme from a match between England and Austria, 7 December 1932 is very collectable despite having a slightly distressed spine. England won 4-3 against the Austrian "Wunderteam" that had remained unbeaten the previous season. The match was close and the Stamford Bridge fans were relieved to hear the final whistle.

£60-80

England International Programmes 3

The first "international" football match organized by the FA was a friendly, played between "Englishmen" and "Scotsmen" at the Kennington Oval on 5 March 1870. England's first recognized international game outside the British Isles did not take place until 6 June 1908 when they played Austria in Vienna. England beat Austria 6-1. This game was part of an England representative side's first tour of Europe which also brought easy wins over Hungary 7-0 and Bohemia 4-0. England's first defeat by a side from outside the British Isles also took place on the Continent when they were defeated 4-3 by Spain in Madrid during May 1929, just a year before the first World Cup. Overseas football match programmes usually follow the same style and size as British examples. However, one small but important difference does exist: England's home international programmes are usually printed partly in the visiting national team's native language which is useful for the travelling supporters. For British fans travelling to games on the Continent, this bi-lingual facility is not often available in the programmes.

◄ During a three-match Continental tour in 1938, England faced Switzerland in Zurich on 21 May. England fielded a strong team, but Switzerland won 2-1. This well-produced 40-page German-text programme, contains action pictures and match reports from many previous European international matches. This publication mistakenly features the British Union flag on the cover instead of the English Cross of St George – a common error on European programmes.

£300-350

▲ The last game in the 1938 England tour (see above), was against France in Paris on 26 May; England won the match 4-2. This large format programme contains a short history of France v England football and a plan of the field of play. Although in poor condition, autographs from both teams seen here on the centre pages, make this piece highly collectable.

£300-350

◄ Another rare and collectable programme, for England's match against Germany in the Olympic Stadium in Berlin on 14 May 1938. The England players were forced to give the Nazi salute – then won 6-3.

£300-400

▼ In a style typical of West German publications of the 1950s and 1960s, this 52-page piece, together with a reproduction of a 1909 England v Germany Amateur International teamsheet, was issued for West Germany's match against England in May 1956. England achieved a magnificent 3-1 victory over the then World Cup holders, with goals from Duncan Edwards (Manchester United), Johnny Haynes (Fulham) and Colin Grainger (Sheffield United).

£40-60

▲ The programme produced for this Denmark v England fixture on 2 October 1955 is compact and basic, and is easily affordable.

£30-40

NEMZETEK KÖZÖTTI VÁLOGATOTT LABDARÚGÓ MÉRKŐZÉS
Budapest, 1954. május 23

Fußball-Länderspiel
Deutschland - England
am Sonnabend, 26. Mai 1956

Preis 30 Pf

▲ An attractive 16-page item, the cover of this programme for England v Hungary match in Budapest on 23 May 1954, appears to portray Ferenc Puskas and Stanley Matthews. England lost this game 7-1.

£100-150

▲ England played France in Paris in May 1949 in the last game of their end-of-season international tour. This 20-page programme, written entirely in French, features picture portraits of the principal French players: Batteux, Gabet, Cuissard, Jonquet, Hon and Salva.

£40-60

Irish International Programmes

Football in Ireland is organized by two governing bodies: the Irish Football Association in Northern Ireland and the Football Association of Ireland in Eire. The first ever Irish international took place between Ireland and England at Belfast in 1882, with a catastrophic 13-0 defeat for the home side. The FAI was formed on 1 June 1921 and played its first home international match on 16 June l924 against the United States in Dublin, where the Irish team celebrated with a good 3-1 win. However, despite the obvious rivalry that exists between the two Associations, Irish International football has often been an interesting mixture of both nations. For example, prior to World War 2, the Northern Irish Football Association regularly selected players from the Irish Republic for its international sides and several Irishmen played for both Northern Ireland and Eire. Attractive and colourful, Irish International programmes are relatively inexpensive to collect.

◄ This programme from England v Ireland, 19 May 1957, is printed in the green of St Patrick and red of St George. It is creased from having been folded in half and has the added authenticity of team changes recorded in ink.

£20-30

◄ Although this attractive programme from Ireland v England, 2 October 1954, has a small tear in the cover, it contains good text by "Ralph of the Rover" – alias W.H. McClatchey of the *Belfast Telegraph*. The Ireland team included the Blanchflower brothers, while England, recently returned from the 1954 World Cup finals in Switzerland, featured the likes of Billy Wright, Stanley Matthews and Don Revie.

£20-40

► After a disastrous World Cup in Brazil, England played this Home International match on 7 October 1950 in Belfast, and managed to beat Ireland 4-1. This programme is in overall good condition.

£20-40

▶ An informative and well-illustrated programme in the colours of the Irish tricolour, from Ireland v Germany on 17 October 1951, this was the first of two international matches between these countries, organized as part of Germany's return to international football. The German team was already regarded as one of Europe's strongest, and included Werner Kohlmeyer, Josef Posipal, Fritz Walter, and Max Morlock, but the Irish achieved an impressive 3-2 victory.

£20-40

▲ A simple, single-sheet piece, this programme was for the Irish Football Association international between Ireland and England, played in Belfast on 28 September 1946. England won the match 7-2. Unfortunately, paper was still rationed, so it has been produced with low quality paper, and also lacks extras such as illustrations.

£30-40

◀ This England-Ireland international on 30 September 1946, was organized to celebrate the Silver Jubilee Year of the formation of the Football Association of Ireland. It was also the first time England had visited Dublin since 1912, when Ireland lost 6-1. Ireland, with Johnny Carey (Manchester United) as captain, were defeated again, 1-0.

£30-50

◀ An amateur international, this match between Eire and Holland was held during the preliminary round of the Olympic Games in 1948. The first since the end of World War 2, they were christened the Austerity Games as rationing was still in force. While most events were based in London, this match was held at the ground of Portsmouth FC. Pieces such as this are rare but not widely collected.

£30-50

▲ These programmes were both issued for Ireland v England on 9 October 1948, the official version published by the Irish FA (left), and an unofficial one (right). Although the lower quality, unofficial piece is rarer, it is not as desirable.

£30-40 official; £15-30 unofficial

Scottish International Programmes

The Scottish Football Association regarded the Scotland v England clash as the greatest of all matches. England was regarded as the "Auld Enemy"! The designs displayed on the Scotland v England match programmes reveal the amount of pride and honour that was at stake. Inside these programmes, the English are playfully referred to as "The Men from the South" or "The Saxons", while the various Scottish teams became "The Wearers of the Thistle". The 1954 match programme included "A Welcome", from the SFA President and secretary, that summed up the unique occasion thus: "We are right glad to see you. We hope you have a fine day … and we hope the Scots will be inspired, the English humbled, and that a great time will be had by all!" The importance of the Scotland v England matches can also be measured by the size and content of the programmes compared to those published for other opponents. Most of the post-war Scotland v England programmes contained an average of 20 pages, but those for non-England games, such as Scotland v Hungary or Scotland v Wales, had only eight pages.

◀ Scotland having qualified for the World Cup finals in Sweden, this game, held on 19 April 1958, was the first of three warm-ups, against England, Hungary and Poland. Sadly Matt Busby had resigned as part-time manager following the Munich plane crash. In this game, Scotland lost 4-0 .

£15-30

◀ The Home International Championship was a very close run thing during the 1955-56 season: before this match on 14 April 1956, England, Scotland, Ireland and Wales had each won and lost one game – in fact all four teams went on to share the trophy, the only time this ever happened!

£20-30

◀ A Home International match/World Cup qualifier held on 3 April 1954, this Scotland-England match was also a battle for inclusion in a "seeded" section of the 1954 World Cup tournament, which was to be hosted by Switzerland. In spite of a good home record against England, Scotland lost this game 4-2.

£30-40

◀ This programme is for the Home International Championship match, which took place on 1 April 1933, during the Diamond Jubilee year of the Scottish Football Association. It has been folded and is creased, and the covers are rather dirty.

£40-60

◀ Played on 10 April 1948, this match was Hampden Park's first Scotland-England international since 1939, with over 500,000 applications for 136,000 tickets! Finney and Mortensen gave England a 2-0 victory.

£30-40

▶ This match on 8 December against Hungary was Scotland's last international match of 1954. The Scottish team had had a poor year, losing in the Home International to England, and facing a series of defeats at the World Cup. The Hungarians had beaten England at their two previous meetings. In spite of a drastically altered Scottish team, the Hungarians won 4-2.

£20-40

▲ Although this Scotland-Wales programme, from 4 November 1959 is relatively short, and has also been folded in half, the footballing names it features make it interesting to collectors. For this match the Scottish side included Dave Mackay, Bobby Evans (captain), Ian St John and Denis Law. Among the Welsh team were Jack Kelsey, Cliff Jones and John Charles. In 1957 Charles had been sold by his team Leeds United to Juventus, for £65,000 – then the highest transfer fee in British football, while Law, in 1961 was to become the first British £100,000 player, when sold by Manchester City to Torino.

£10-20

▶ In 1950 the World Cup Organising Committee decided that two British teams should go to the World Cup finals in Brazil, but Scotland stated they would only go as Home Champions. Roy Bentley's goal in the match held on 15 April 1950 meant that Scotland stayed at home while England went to Rio.

£30-40

Welsh International Programmes

The Football Association of Wales was formed in 1876. A band of Welsh amateur players, led by Llewelyn Kenrick, bravely challenged the Scottish FA to play a match against Wales under Association rules. The challenge was accepted and a Welsh team travelled to Glasgow. Wales lost her first international 4-0. International games between England and Wales have been played since 1879 and Mr Kenrick must have been a proud man as a member of the first Welsh eleven to defeat England at Blackburn in 1881. Despite this famous victory, Wales has often been confined to an inferior status and treated with a certain amount of contempt as a footballing nation. Indeed, during the 1890s the Football Association even sent an England second eleven to play Wales on the same day as England were playing Ireland! Most Welsh international programmes produced throughout the 1940s and 1950s were printed in Cardiff by E. Davies & Sons. Later editions were printed by David Printers Ltd, and Provincial Printing & Publishing Co Ltd. They all tend to be small and fairly subdued publications without the colour of English international programmes, or the bright nationalist humour and razzamatazz portrayed so vividly in Scottish examples.

► A small programme from Wales v England 16 November 1932, this piece contains facts about the teams and pictures of the star players. This great Welsh side won the Home Championship this season and the next.

£80-120

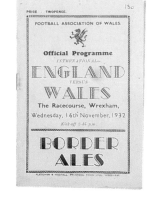

◄ This Wales v England fixture, played on 15 October 1949, marked for both sides the beginning of the World Cup as FIFA had decided that the Home International Championship should be used as a qualifying tournament. This programme is in good condition, it is clean and uncreased, though the staple in its spine has rusted.

£20-40

► Wales v England, held on 20 October 1951 was Wales' first international match of this season. It was the 62nd Wales v England game to date. The match ended in a 1-1 draw, and this season these two teams shared the Home International Championship.

£15-30

1102

▼ Wales v England, 19 October 1957, was Wales' sixth international match of 1957; they had played four 1958 World Cup competition qualifying games against Czechoslovakia and East Germany. The Welsh had an unhappy game and lost 4-0 to England on this occasion. This programme has a typical crease running through it from being folded in half. However it does benefit from having a *Western Mail* pre-match song sheet which includes: *Men of Harlech, Calon Lan, We'll Keep a Welcome, Sospan Fach, Cwm Rhondda* and *Aberystwyth*.

£15-30

▼ Another simple eight-page programme, this example from Wales v England, 18 October 1947, was published while paper was still rationed. England, who at the time were almost invincible, won 3-0.

£20-40

▲ 1951 marked the 75th anniversary of the Welsh FA and this match, on 5 December 1951, against the Rest of the United Kingdom, was staged to celebrate "a great occasion in the history of Welsh Football". The opposition included English, Scottish and Irish internationals, but Wales won 3-2. This official programme is unusual because four pages remain uncut.

£15-30

► Following a successful summer at the World Cup in 1958 where they reached the quarter-finals, finally losing 1-0 to Brazil, the future Champions for that year, Wales were beaten on 18 October by a strong Scottish side that featured Dennis Law and Tommy Docherty.

£15-30

◄ The Home International game against England on 10 October 1953 was one Wales desperately wanted to win having been in wooden spoon position after the 1952-53 Championship season. They losy 4-1. This is a complimentary copy with a red cord binding.

£15-30

Wartime International Programmes

The first wartime international match was played between Wales and England on 11 November 1939 at Cardiff in aid of Red Cross funds. The result was a 1-1 draw in front of a crowd of 28,000 spectators who raised £1,406. Two weeks later in a return game at the Racehorse Ground, Wrexham, the England XI, which was trailing by two goals at half-time, won 3-2 after second-half goals by Martin and Balmer, and a Welsh own goal. After the declaration of war, one of the Government's initial fears was that large crowds gathering at football matches presented the possible danger of heavy casualties in the event of an air raid. Therefore these first two wartime internationals were played in

Wales because it was deemed to be a "safe" area. Some of the wartime internationals were curious affairs. For example, on 25 September 1943, England beat Wales 8-3 at Wembley. Early in the match Wales were reduced to ten men due to injuries, so Stanley Mortensen, an England reserve, made his (unofficial) international debut as a substitute wearing the red jersey of Wales!

◀ Because of paper rationing this simple programme from 17 April 1943, Scotland v England, is a single sheet, printed on both sides, and folded into three sections. At Hampden Park a crowd of 105,000 watched England win 4-0. An inexperienced Scottish side including George Young, Sammy Kean and Willie Buchan, faced a well-established England team, with Swift, Mercer and Matthews.

£30-50

◀ Another single-sheet, "four-page" programme, for the England v Scotland match of 16 October 1943, has been folded and is therefore not in good condition. However, it probably belonged to a sports correspondent because it contains some interesting comments on England's 8-0 victory written in pencil on the back. This was the first of two England-Scotland wartime internationals to be played in Manchester; the second, called a "Victory International", was held on 24 August 1946.

£20-40

▼ This England-Wales match held on 16 September 1944, was the first real (though unofficial) international to be played in Liverpool since 1935. The fixture resulted in a 2-2 draw, with Carter, Lawton, Dearson and Lucas scoring a goal apiece.

£20-40

◀ This programme from England v Belgium, 19 January 1946, salutes the Belgian team for resuming play so soon after experiencing "five long years of German occupation". This was Billy Wright's first England match, and the home side won 2-0.

£20-40

▶ Held on 14 October 1944, this match was the fourth England v Scotland wartime international at Wembley since 1939, and the thirteenth meeting since the outbreak of the war. Tommy Lawton's hat-trick helped England to a 6-2 victory.

£20-40

▼ In this match at Villa Park, 3 February 1945, England (captained by Joe Mercer) beat Scotland (led by Matt Busby) 3-2 in front of 66,000 people who had paid £17,799 – a wartime record at the time. This was the second wartime international to be staged in Birmingham (the first having been played in 1941 at St Andrews).

£20-30

▶ The programme for this Victory International between Scotland and England, 13 April 1946, contains a Roll of Honour as a "tribute to the footballers who laid down their lives for their country" A record crowd for the 1939-46 period of around 140,000, watched Scotland beat England 1-0. Hampden Park also staged the last Victory International, Scotland v Switzerland, in May 1946.

£30-50

▶ This programme for England v France, 26 May 1945, features a message to the Federation Française de Football that reads: "We can imagine nothing more appropriate than that our old friends and allies from France should participate ... in the first ... match played in this country since the unconditional surrender of our enemy in Europe." The final score was 2-2.

£30-50

European Competition Programmes

Ever since the mid-1950s and early 1960s British clubs have been taking part in European competitions. The European Champions Cup, better known as the European Cup, began in 1955-56 and soon established itself as the primary club competition in the world. Manchester United became the first English club to go into the European Cup in 1956-57, because Chelsea, League champions in 1954-55, had refused the invitation to compete. The European Cup Winners Cup, which involves the winners of Europe's knockout competitions, began in 1960-61, with Wolverhampton Wanderers and Rangers representing British hopes. The UEFA Cup, Europe's third major competition got under way in 1971-72, growing out of the old Inter-Cities Fairs Cup, which had been held since 1953-54. Qualification is by various routes. The Super Cup has been contested by the winners of the European Cup and the holders of the European Cup Winners Cup since 1972. The programmes published for the matches by the clubs involved in European competitions are generally good quality, and are also still quite easily obtainable.

▼ Four British teams took part in the 1961-62 European Cup. This programme is from Rangers' quarter-final second-leg match against Standard Liège of Belgium. Rangers had lost the first leg 4-1, and only managed to achieve a 2-0 win in the second, losing 4-3 on aggregate.

£5-15

SOUVENIR PROGRAMME

EUROPEAN CUP TOURNAMENT FOR LEAGUE CHAMPIONS
QUARTER-FINAL
SECOND TIE

THE RANGERS v

STANDARD LIEGE

6D   WEDNESDAY, FEBRUARY 14, 1962 Kick-off 7.30 p.m.
IBROX STADIUM · GLASGOW

▼ Both rare and collectable, this programme is from the quarter-final second-leg European Cup match between Red Star Belgrade and Manchester United, in Yugoslavia, on 5 February 1958. United finished this round 5-4 on aggregate. Sadly the plane taking the team back to England the next day crashed, killing 23 people, including eight players. This programme has been reproduced, so be cautious when collecting.

£300-500

KUP EVROPSKIH FUTBALSKIH ŠAMPIONA
„Manchester united"

„Cevena zvezda"
5-II-1958
Stadion JNA

▶ Issued in 1957, this rare European Cup programme is from a match between Manchester United and Dukla Prague, on 4 December. In the following round came United's disaster at Munich (see above).

£40-60

Sportem k rozvijení přátelství mezi národy
Let's strenghten all nations sport friendship

BEER

DUKLA PRAHA
MANCHESTER UNITED

▲ As winners of the Welsh Cup in 1967, Cardiff City qualified to participate in the 1967-68 European Cup Winners Cup, and reached the semi-final.

£20-30

▲ This 12-page souvenir programme was issued for Rangers' preliminary round first-leg European Cup match against Real Madrid, at Ibrox stadium, Glasgow, on 25 September 1963. They lost this match 1-0.

£10-15

▼ Produced in Italy, this programme was issued for Inter-Milan's European Cup semi-final second-leg game against Liverpool, on 12 May 1965. After winning the first leg at Anfield, Liverpool were beaten 4-3 on aggregate after Inter's 3-0 victory in this match. Inter went on to beat Benfica 1-0 in the final.

£15-30

► Jock Stein's Celtic team were competing in the European Cup competition for the first time in 1966-67. This illustrated 12-page, souvenir programme is from the semi-final first leg match against Dukla Prague, the Czechoslovakian Army side, at Celtic Park, Glasgow, on 12 April 1967, which Celtic won 3-1. Celtic then went on to become the first British club to win the European Cup when they defeated Inter-Milan 2-1 in Lisbon, on 25 May 1967.

£15-20

▲ Manchester United became the first English club to win the European Cup in 1967-68 season when they beat Benfica 4-1 after extra time, on 29 May 1968. On three previous occasions (1957, 1958 and 1966) the team had got as far as the semi-finals. This official *United Review* programme is from the second round second-leg match against FK Sarajevo, in which United achieved a narrow 2-1 victory.

£20-30

43

Books & Publications

Both active and armchair sportsmen are spoilt for choice when it comes to publications on their favourite sport. Every year, particularly around Christmas time, books appear in bookshops all over the country, dedicated to sports of every kind. Football books are amongst the most popular of these, with annuals, year books, club histories and autobiographies all competing with each other for sales.

Some of these publications have been favourites every year for decades and are almost household names, such as *News of the World Football Annual*, *Rothman's Football Yearbook*, and *SHOOT Annual*. Others are written by players, managers, referees and other personalities of the soccer world, capitalizing on their popularity or notoriety at the time. These may be accounts of conventional careers in football, or fascinating histories featuring sensational revelations and interesting opinions of the game.

Similarly, every week or month, a colourful selection of football-related magazines and periodicals are displayed for sale on the shelves of newsagents. All ages are catered for, from "Roy of the Rovers"-style comics to glossy and expensive football magazines printed on high-quality art paper. Football magazines, especially the more serious and better-written titles, can be collected week-by-week or month-by-month to form an encyclopedia of soccer with each season's tale of League Championship, Cup competitions and international campaigns, unfolding issue by issue. In this respect the contents of football magazines and periodicals are often more immediate and spontaneous than books on the subject, as well as better illustrated. Older examples, particularly late 1940s publications, though not as sophisticated as today's magazines, still manage to reveal football as it was played during a golden age. The paper on which these magazines and periodicals were printed may have become yellowed and brittle with age, but the football remains as magnificent as it ever was.

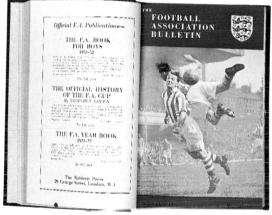

Football clubs also publish their own magazines and periodicals – the match day programme being akin to a magazine and the periodicals taking the form of official seasonal souvenirs and handbooks. Dedicated followers of football have an inexhaustible appetite for these publications. Handbooks, published by most football clubs for many years, come out prior to each football season and contain essential dates and information such as fixture lists of forthcoming matches, details of players and staff, and facts and figures from the previous season. These handbooks are mainly of academic interest and are still inexpensive to collect. Official souvenirs, on the other hand, are often colourful celebratory publications, compiled and written by clubs to commemorate league or cup success. These are as sought after as the corresponding match day programmes issued for the same games or competitions.

Football has a long history, much of it recorded in the written word and presented in the form of short-span publications, including year books, annuals, autobiographies, magazines, handbooks and souvenirs. A collection of these provides an invaluable and unique knowledge of the game.

Left: David Miller's official Football Association account of the 1970 World Cup. *Background image:* The *Athletic News Football Annual* for 1919-20, the first season after World War 1. *Above:* The *Football Association Bulletin,* here bound into an annual volume, was the FA's official journal for many seasons.

Books 1

Unlike Britain's other so-called national sports such as cricket and golf, the popular game of football did not spawn much literature of quality in its early days. Whereas the other sports were responsible for many well written and sometimes expensively produced titles during the 19th and early 20th centuries, which are excellent for history and reference, similar volumes devoted to the game of football are unfortunately rare. In the introduction to *Association Football & The Men Who Made It* (1907), Alfred Gibson and William Pickford point out that: "So far Association Football has had no voice commensurate with its claims. During the last 20 years the game has developed in such a remarkable manner that literature on the subject has failed to keep pace with it … It is with the desire to supply in some measure the urgent needs of the age that this book has been produced." Indeed, apart from this book, most "old" or "collectable" football literature available today dates from as recently as the 1940s and 1950s, in the post-war boom of football in Britain.

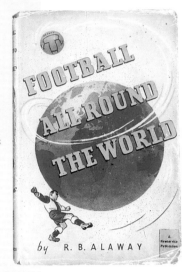

◄ Bob Alaway's *Football All Round The World* (1948), a story of world football from 1900, was a limited edition available to subscribers only. R.B. Alaway was a recognized authority on amateur and international soccer. This dust-jacketed example has a signed dedication from the author in ink, dated January 1948.

£30-40

► *Chelsea Champions! 50 years of Chelsea Football* is a good example of the popular literature published to celebrate the game of football. This example is in good condition, and is complete with its dust jacket.

£10-15

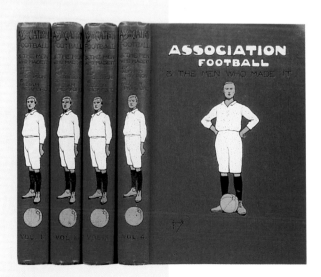

◄ *Association Football & The Men Who Made It* (1907) in four volumes, is the corner stone of any collection of football books, and can be regarded as one of the first 20th century literary works on the game. This set of volumes is complete with all 97 illustration plates and is in good, clean condition.

£200-300

◄ *The Wolves – The First Eighty Years* (1959) by Percy M. Young is a good club history. This one is in good condition, with its dust jacket. It is made more collectable by an inscription from the author on the title page.

£10-15

◄ Bound in blue half calf leather and gilt, this volume from 1904 written by the Duke of Beaufort, and bound in leather and gilt, is one of a long line of Badminton Library books on football, first published in 1887.

£50-80

► *The Story of the Football League 1888-1938* (1938) is an official history published in commemoration of the 50th anniversary of its formation, compiled by Charles E. Sutcliffe, J. A. Brierley, and F. Howarth. This example is a Second Edition, published in February 1939, with its dust jacket and is in very good condition.

£80-120

▼ *My Twenty Years of Soccer* (1955) by Tommy Lawton concerns the glittering football career of this popular player who became a professional at the age of 17. Books such as this provide the collector with first-hand accounts from football's star players about their experiences, and their opinions of the game and fellow professionals.

£15-20

▼ Another essential part of any collection, *Association Football* (1960) edited by A.H. Fabian & Geoffrey Green contains contributions from numerous prominent football writers of the day. This first edition set of four volumes is complete with all four colour frontispiece illustrations.

£100-200

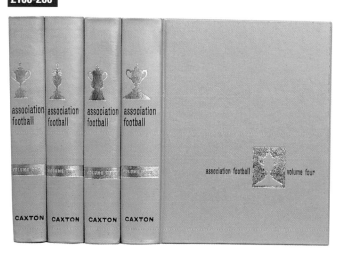

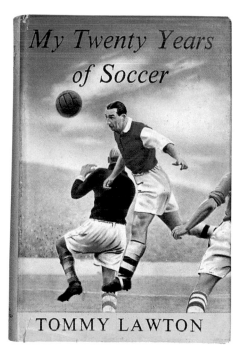

Books 2

No collection of football memorabilia is complete without a selection of good books to chronicle the history of the game and celebrate the characters that formed it. Because football has changed considerably over the years, it is interesting today for collectors and football historians to read contemporary views and reports on the game. The issues concerning football writers and football commentators since the formation of the Football Association in 1863 and the Football League was founded in 1888 have included the transfer system; the Players' Union and the threatened strike of 1910; throw-in reform; the controversy of the two-referees plan in 1935; the Pools controversy; the application from the BBC to broadcast League matches; the decision to rejoin FIFA and the World Cup, etc. It is possible to learn about these and other important topics from modern books written with the benefit of hind-sight; however older contemporary literature is more immediate and often contains the seeds of ideas later adopted by the games' governing bodies. It also reflects the problems experienced by those implementing change.

► This book by John Allan is packed full of records and statistics. This copy is a very collectable example as it has a dust jacket in good condition, together with a folder containing the club's League results 1890-1934.

£40-60

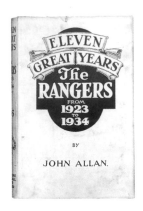

► Although better known as a cricket writer, John Arlott's *Concerning Soccer* was first published in 1952. Arlott was very interested in soccer, and this book is informed and readable.

£10-20

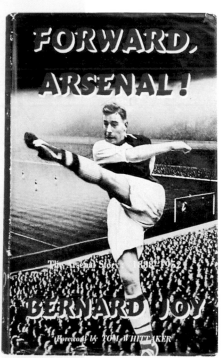

◄ *Forward, Arsenal! – The Arsenal Story 1888-1952* (1952), written by Bernard Joy, Football Correspondent for *The Star*, has a foreword by Tom Whittaker (1920s player, later trainer and manager at Highbury). Arsenal is one of the most written about football clubs, and this example is one of the best popular works of its period. Bernard Joy was a member of the Arsenal team during some of its greatest days, and also played for England.

£15-20

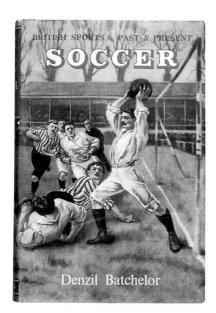

◀ *The Football League 1888-1988, The Official Illustrated History* (1987) by Byron Butler is a corner-stone for any collection. In 1988 the Football League, the oldest competition of its kind in the world, was 100 years old and this book is an official celebration of that occasion with over 350 pages. Bryon Butler is BBC Radio's football correspondent.

£5-15

▲ *British Sports Past & Present – Soccer* (1954) by Denzil Batchelor was written at a time when Wolves and Hungary were the teams others tried to emulate, and players such as Tom Finney, Stanley Matthews and Billy Wright were household names. The author was Sports Editor of *Picture Post* and a regular contributor to BBC sporting programmes. This copy is a good example; the dust jacket is reproduced from a painting by W.H. Overend showing a match in 1890.

£10-15

◀ *Feet First*, Stanley Matthews' autobiography first published in 1948, is both a personal history and a coaching manual. *Feet First Again* (1952) updates the story.

£20-30 for the pair

▶ Two official FA publications from the 1950s, both produced with Walter Winterbottom, who was appointed Director of Coaching by the FA in 1946, and England team manager.

£20-30 for the pair

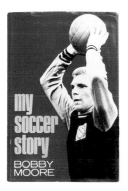  

◀ This review copy of *Bobby Moore: My Soccer Story* (1966) is signed by ten West Ham players including Martin Peters, John Sissons and Ron Boyce. In 1966 at the age of only 25 Bobby Moore was the golden boy of football, and remained one of the sport's most admired players. Sadly he died in 1993.

£30-40

Books 3

Books occupy a special place amongst the collectors of football memorabilia. even more than other publications such as programmes and periodicals, books are the favourite means by which football history, literature and information is recorded and transmitted. These books – regardless of their age – are likely to be read, and unlike other football collectables and works of art which may remain untouched in cabinets or albums, will suffer from handling by successive readers. However, despite the inevitability of use, there are a number of simple precautions that collectors can take to protect and prolong the life of books.

* Keep books dry and in constant cool conditions – away from direct central heating which can dry books out resulting in warping and cracking.

* If possible, store books away from direct sunlight to protect coloured covers and dust jackets from fading.

* Open books carefully – some hinges and joints will crack if a book is opened unnecessarily widely.

* Don't pack books too tightly in a book-case or on a shelf and avoid removing them by hooking a finger over the top of the spine as this will eventually weaken the binding.

▶ *Spurs – The Complete Official Story of Tottenham Hotspur FC* (1956) by Julian Holland, is related partly through the memories of ex-Spurs players, including Bobby Buckle from the 1880s, and Arthur Grimsdell, captain in the 1920s.

£5-10

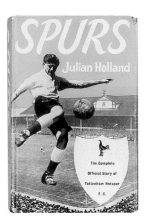

▶ The purpose of *Constructive Football* (1950) by A.H. Fabian and Tom Whittaker, was to enable young players to improve their technique, as well as to help spectators achieve a greater appreciation of the game.

£10-15

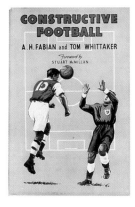

◀ Tommy Lawton's *Football Is My Business* (1946), a small autobiographical book, was written when Lawton, "England's dynamic young centre-forward", was still only 26. It is the first part of the dramatic story of one of England's best forwards, who began playing League football in 1935 when he was only 16. He scored 22 goals in 23 matches for England, each side of the war.

£10-15

▲ This first edition in good condition of the *King of Soccer* (1957) by John Charles, plots the career of Charles, "the gentle giant" of Welsh and later Italian football.

£10-15

▼ Jimmy Greaves published his first autobiography in 1962 when he was only 23, and had just signed to play for Tottenham Hotspur.

£15-30

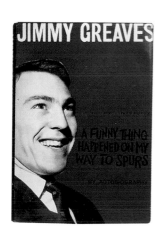

▼ *Captain of Hungary* (1955), tells the story of Ferenc Puskas, the "Galloping Major", captain of the side who beat England 6-3 at Wembley in 1953. Puskas later played for the Spanish national team.

£20-40

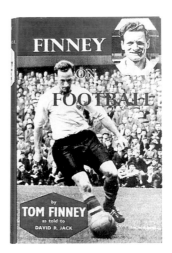

▲ The "Preston Plumber" Tom Finney's second book, *Finney on Football* (1958), deals with many topics of interest and controversy that were important in the soccer world during the late 1950s, and also remain relevant today.

£10-15

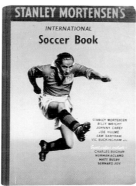  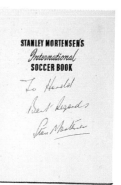

▲ Stanley Mortensen wrote his *International Soccer Book* in the early 1950S. This slightly battered example has been signed by the author. In this book, Mortensen and other famous stars of the period tell of their experiences in international soccer. The book also contains colour portraits of over 50 International players from England, Scotland, Ireland and Wales.

£50-80

Books 4

Football books remain plentiful and relatively inexpensive. Most of the examples featured on these pages can be discovered upon the shelves of second-hand bookshops, while usually priced at less than £30. It is therefore possible for collectors to be cautious about price and choosy about condition when buying and collecting. Dust-jackets, illustrations, pages and bindings, together with the overall condition and complete-ness, should all be checked. It is often a good idea to specialize. Player's biographies and autobiographies make up the largest group, especially from the 1950s to the present day, and may have the added attraction of being signed by the personality or author. Club histories are essential to collections, and early publications often include information, facts and anecdotes that similar, later and more up-to-date examples may choose to omit. The popular soccer annuals are probably amongst the more enjoyable and readable of all the football books, with "Boys' Book" types rapidly increasing in value because of interest from collectors of toys and juvenilia.

▶ Typical of the period, this autobiography, *Captain of England*, from 1950 relates the climb of Billy Wright, then aged only 26, to the top of the footballing ladder, as captain of Wolverhampton Wanderers and England, a post he had just achieved.

£10-15

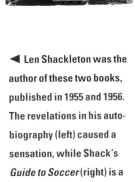

◀ Len Shackleton was the author of these two books, published in 1955 and 1956. The revelations in his auto-biography (left) caused a sensation, while Shack's *Guide to Soccer* (right) is a humorous look at the game.

£15-25 each

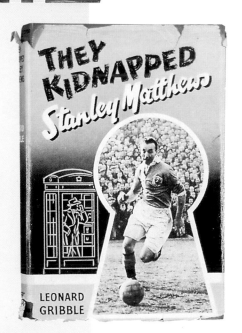

◀ A fictional detective story first published in 1950, *They Kidnapped Stanley Matthews – A Case for Superintendent Anthony Slade* by Leonard Gribble, features Stanley Matthews as a guest character. The story was written with the player's co-operation and through the tale the reader is introduced to the Matthews family and taken into the hotel he owns in Blackpool.

£10-20

◀ This 1974 edition of the *Scorcher Annual*, published by IPC Magazines in 1973, is a mixture of comic-strip stories, football quizzes and features on leading players and clubs. Children's books such as this are becoming increasingly popular.

£5-15

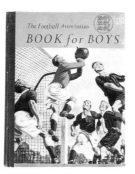

▲ *The FA Book for Boys* was a good quality series published during the "golden years" of the game, this example from 1949 is the second edition. The introduction is written by Stanley Rous, secretary of the FA, and the contents include contributions by many respected football names of the time: Stan Mortensen, Charles Buchan, Tom Finney, John Arlott and Joe Mercer. It is highly illustrated with photographs and cartoons.

£15-30

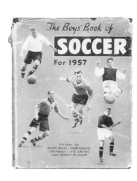

▲ A typical boys' football annual of the 1950s *The Boys' Book of Soccer* (1957), first published in 1956, is an interesting and entertaining mixture of football facts and fiction. There are League and International reports, as well as instructive articles by well-known names that include John Charles (Leeds United) and Roger Byrne (Manchester United). The dust jacket on this example is untidy and worn which will reduce its value.

£15-30

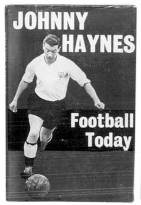

▲ These two books from 1961 and 1962 give an account of the career of Johnny Haynes, captain of Fulham and England, the first £100-a-week player, and a respected football personality.

£15-30 each

▶ *Football From The Goalmouth* (1948) by Frank Swift and *Footballer's Progress* (1950) by Raich Carter are two autobiographical titles published by Sporting Handbooks Ltd. Frank Swift tells of his rise from young Blackpool boatman to England's first-choice goalkeeper after World War 2. Sadly he died in the 1958 Munich air crash while working as a journalist. Raich Carter details the ups and downs of a professional footballer's career – as a player with Sunderland, Derby County, Hull City and England, and also as a manager.

£10-15 each

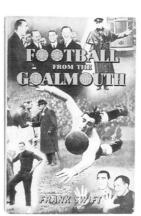
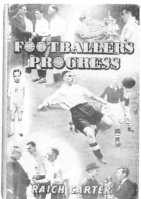

Yearbooks & Annuals 1

Yearbooks and annuals are an important part of most football fans' literature and go hand-in-hand with football programmes and official club handbooks. Almost all are published prior to each football season, and contain essential information about the forthcoming season's fixtures, together with other important dates and the Football Association's diary of events. Contents in addition to this depend on the publisher. For example, those editions that are published provincially, and whose parent newspapers follow the local football teams, often exclusively feature those clubs' previous seasons progress, list their players and generally provide information for the fans. On the other hand, some are simply vehicles for entrepreneur sports-shop owners to advertise their products, while others were published privately by bookmakers as incentives to romote betting and gambling! Collectors often go for the better annuals and yearbooks, such as *The Athletic News*, *Sunday Chronicle*, *Empire News*, and *News of the World Annuals*, or *Rothmans Football Yearbooks*, for the same reason as collectors of cricketana eagerly await the publication of each year's edition of *Wisden's Cricketers' Almanack*.

◀ *The Topical Times Football Annual* was produced in association with the hugely popular *Topical Times* weekly sports paper. The price shown here is for 15 volumes, 1925-26 to 1939-40.

£80-120

▶ **This early annual from 1912-13 was published by Birmingham-based football outfitter William Shillcock, giving him the chance to advertise his stock in his own publication.**

£30-40

▼ **The Rothmans series of yearbooks, first published in 1970, have become popular amongst keen followers of the game as well as collectors of football books and memorabilia. Most years of this handbook are still available at secondhand bookshops and make a good addition to any collection.**

£100-150 for a complete run

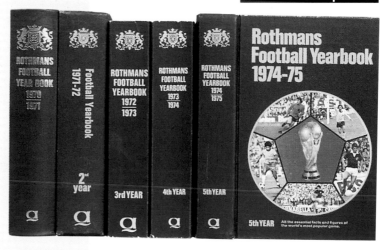

▼ The *Daily Mail Football Guide* is likely to be of great interest to collectors of football memorabilia. In the 1950-51 edition, one of the important developments to deserve mention was the 40 shilling-a-week pay rise that allowed top-wage professionals to earn a new maximum wage of £14 a week! Because of the resources available these *Football Guides* are extremely well written and professionally produced with numerous illustrations and charts. A typical example includes fixtures for the season, soccer prospects, Scottish football, International results, FA Cup, League tables and results and amateur and minor leagues. This price is for 22 volumes, from 1951-52 to 1972-73.

£80-120

▲ The *Football Association Yearbook* has been published since the 1948-49 season and is a good guide to the organization of the game in Britain, as well as an account of the past season's matches. Published as paperbacks, collectors can expect to find older copies bound in volumes with hard covers.

£200-300 for a complete run

▼ The *Sports Argus Football Annual – The Midlands' Own Football Annual* was published over many years by the *Birmingham Gazette* and the *Birmingham Evening Mail & Despatch*. This is an interesting series of informative annuals that is proud and enthusiastic about all types and levels of football in the Midlands, featuring teams such as Aston Villa, West Bromwich Albion, Birmingham City, Coventry City, Wolverhampton Wanderers and Walsall, together with Midland fixtures, Southern and West Midlands Leagues, Midland Clubs' Full Cup Records, and Midlands Schools Football, as well as details of local minor clubs. The price featured here is for a set of 19 volumes, from 1949-50 to 1967-68.

£50-80

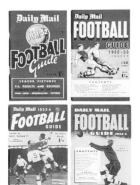

▲ The *Daily Worker Football Annual* never enjoyed the nationwide success that others did, but is collectable nevertheless. This group contains articles by personalities including Matt Busby, Frank Soo and Billy Liddell.

£10-15 each

▲ These four volumes of the *Daily News Football Annual* 1920-21 to 1923-24 include the usual table of contents such as the fixture list for all the main leagues. Also featured are referees, players, and the laws of the game.

£60-80

Yearbooks & Annuals 2

When a soccer historian or collector of football memorabilia needs to know specific information or facts concerning the teams, players and results of football clubs or national sides, together with league tables, fixture lists and results, he or she will turn to one of the many football annuals and yearbooks – but usually to either The *Athletic News/ Sunday Chronicle/ Empire News & Sunday Chronicle/ News of the World* editions or, the more recent, *Rothmans Football Yearbooks*. In 1986-87 the *News of the World Football Annual* became the first in its field to reach the 100th edition. The original issue, published published in 1887, was a 16-page pamphlet, *The Athletic News Supplement and Club Directory*. By 1890, with the Football League celebrating its second anniversary, it was published in book form. *The Athletic News Football Annual* was football's "Bible" for many years, during which it spawned many imitators in both content and style. The first *Rothmans Football Yearbook* was published in September 1970 for the 1970-71 season. This important series of yearbooks is essential for collectors of soccer memorabilia, although older examples are often in poor condition. Many collectors purchase two copies at a time, one for reading and research and one to keep in perfect condition.

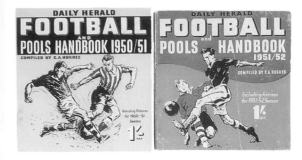

▲ The *Daily Herald Football and Pools Handbook* features reviews of the seasons of all the British leagues, and a host of other articles, as well as a comprehensive list of contents including facts and figures concerning English and Scottish Leagues, internationals and amateur clubs.

£25-35 for four volumes 1950-51 to 1953-54

▲ Within its 64 pages, the *Winner Football Annual 1927-28*, includes a full listing of all English Football League fixtures together with international and Cup dates.

£15-30

▼ Watford Football Club was founded in 1898 and by the 1933-34 season they were in the Division 3 (South) and, like many smaller League clubs, were in financial trouble. This illustrated handbook, the *Watford Observer Football Handbook*, looks forward to better luck in the new season.

£15-30

◄ For most soccer fans and collectors the *Athletic News Football Annual* is football's equivalent of *Wisden's Cricketer's Almanack*. First published in 1887, it set the standards and style that numerous other similar publications have attempted to emulate. After a number of name changes (the *Sunday Chronicle Football Album*, the *Empire News & Sunday Chronicle – The Two in One Football Annual*, the *News of the World & Empire News – The Two in One Football Annual*), the book became the *News of the World Football Annual* in 1965-66, a title by which it is still known today. Very early editions of this annual, particularly pre-1900, are now quite difficult to find and facsimiles do exist for those collectors keen to acquire a complete set.

£4,000 for 105 volumes

▼ The *Evening Dispatch Football Handbook 1949-50* almost exclusively features Scottish football, with details of all the Scottish Leagues and fixtures. Scotland had won the Home International Championship in 1949 and the nation was looking forward to another successful football season.

£5-10

▲ *Racing & Football Outlook's Football Annual* was designed to be an aid to betting on the football pools. They now give collectors a gambler's insight into past performances of teams and players season by season. The price given here is for seven editions 1953-59.

£30-50

▼ Two editions of the *Sports Mercury Football Annual*, for the 1921-22 and 1922-23 seasons, that deal with all levels of Association Football and Rugby Football in Leicestershire. At the time Leicester City were in Division 2, having renamed themselves after being Leicester Fosse since 1884.

£15-30 each

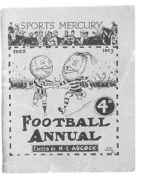

Football Club Handbooks

Fans and followers of football clubs have always been keen for literature on their chosen club or clubs. Match programmes are the obvious example of this, but close on their heels are official handbooks published by the Football Clubs or Supporters' Clubs affiliated to the teams. The original purpose of these handbooks was as fixture lists at the turn of the 20th century, but they soon developed into brochures containing messages from the club chairmen and managers, pictures of staff and players, statistics and post-mortems on previous seasons' performances, results and fixtures. These booklets give an interesting insight into the theories and aspirations of the clubs. Until recently these small handbooks, which often have unassuming covers, were largely overlooked by collectors (often seduced by the growing interest in match programmes). However, they are nearly always worth reading and collecting.

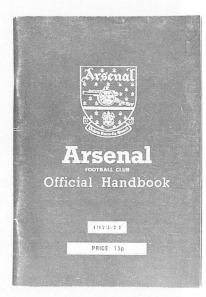

▶ Formed in 1905, Chelsea FC reached Division 1 of the Football League by 1907. This rare, 64-page pocket-sized official handbook is for the 1914-15 season, the last before World War 1. Chelsea finished second from bottom.

£30-40

▼ Charlton Athletic FC were in Division 2 for the 1932-33 season, and the mood of the club and its supporters was generally optimistic. Unfortunately the club finished bottom of Division 2 and were relegated.

£10-15

▲ English League football during the 1930s was dominated by Arsenal Football Club and their innovative manager, Herbert Chapman. Arsenal were League champions five times (1931, 1933, 1934, 1935, 1938), and FA Cup winners twice (1930, 1936). The two handbooks (above) are typical of this period. The larger-format handbook (above left) is from the 1973-74 season.

£5-15 each

► Both issued by Fulham FC, the handbook (right) was produced in 1934-35 while the club was a member of Division 2. The larger, more colourful yearbook (far right) celebrates Fulham's first season in Division 1 in 1949-50. With a large number of features and illustrations, it is more in keeping with publications associated with larger British teams.

£15-20 each

▲ Published for the season 1933-34, this West Ham United annual handbook gives an excellent insight into football at the club during the 1930s, including pictures, facts and figures.

£15-20

▼ This well-produced 56-page handbook was published by the Crystal Palace FC Supporters' Club for 1937-38.

£15-30

◄ These four consecutive Tottenham handbooks come from the mid to late 1930s when the team was in Division 2. The 1935-36 publication discusses the team's recent relegation from Division 1. The 1939-40 edition is interesting because it anticipated a season which was abandoned after just three matches because of the outbreak of World War 2. With other clubs, Spurs were temporarily expelled from the League in 1941.

£10-15 each

► Queen's Park Rangers were a Division 3 (South) club for the 1938-39 season. The handbook produced for that season (right) describes plans to build a new stand at the club's ground. The 1969-70 edition (far right) was the first example of a new-style handbook produced while QPR was a Division 2 club.

£5-15 each

Official Club Publications

Football Clubs that publish or commission "official" publications and souvenirs usually do so to commemorate a special event or footballing success. They are usually well presented with interesting text and a good selection of illustrations and sometimes cartoons. The attraction of these publications is that they are often written to coincide with, or shortly before or after, the event they were intended to celebrate, and as a result, the text reflects the pride, excitement or joy experienced by the club involved. In this respect they are a great deal more lively to read than many contemporary programmes and books, so that today's collectors can enjoy some of the atmostphere and flavour of the occasions from studying them. Collectors may also learn something of the wealth and social importance of a club or the effect the club's achievements had on that season's football, from reading and comparing these official club publications. For example, it speaks volumes about Arsenal Football Club's reputation in the 1930s, that HRH the Prince of Wales consented to inaugurate the new buildings of the Arsenal Stadium.

► Published during August 1950, *The Story of Port Vale 1876-1950* commemorates the opening of the club's new ground at Hamil Road, Burslem, and features plans and illustrations of the finished complex.

£5-15

▼ The 60 pages of this club souvenir record the 25-year history of the Southampton Supporters Club 1926-51, and was issued with the aims of stimulating support for the Saints, and success for the game in general.

£10-15

▲ This typically well-produced Arsenal booklet was published to commemorate the opening of the West Stand by HRH The Prince of Wales in 1932, and the inaugural match against Chelsea. It contains plans and illustrations showing the evolution of the ground after the team moved to Highbury in 1913. The popularity of Arsenal makes this piece very collectable.

£40-60

◄ An important item of non-League memorabilia, this piece records highlights of Hereford's epic FA Cup run during the 1971-72 season. The team reached the fourth round (beating Division I Newcastle in the first round), before losing to West Ham in a replay.

£2-5

▲ Hibernian won the Scottish League in 1947-48, breaking the Rangers-Celtic monopoly. This souvenir was issued to celebrate the achievement, and also to pay tribute to ex-manager Willie McCartney who had recently died. Although an interesting piece, this example is in poor condition.

£10-15

▼ Produced to commemorate Manchester United reaching the FA Cup Final in 1962-63 against Leicester City, *The Reds at Wembley* contains text by Matt Busby, Denis Law, Bobby Charlton and Noel Cantwell.

£15-20

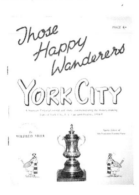

▲ *York City - Those Happy Wanderers* captures the then Division 3 (North) team's excitement at the prospect of their FA Cup semi-final against Newcastle United on 26 March 1955. York City scored first in the initial 1-1 draw, before eventually losing in the replay.

£20-40

▲ Produced by the *Weekly Herald* with the approval and co-operation of Tottenham Hotspur FC, this booklet was compiled from action photographs and cartoons of Spurs players during the 1962-63 season. The cover shows the jubilant Cup Winners Cup-winning Spurs side that defeated Atletico Madrid 5-1 in Rotterdam on 15 May 1963. Jimmy Greaves and Terry Dyson both scored twice, with one goal from John White.

£5-10

Souvenir Publications

The popularity of football means that there is large number of souvenir literature and annuals available for collectors of all teams and countries. This was particularly true of souvenir football literature published during some of the boom years of football during the 1930s and 1950s. Most of this literature, which is usually well-written and illustrated with photographs, provides collectors of football memorabilia with fascinating contemporary insights into the game. The literature was never very expensive, usually costing no more than a few old pence, and so today tends to be equally inexpensive to buy. Collectors can often find these souvenirs and annuals in a host of places, from jumble sales and charity shops, to second-hand bookshops and dealers of sports memorabilia. The cost of these items depends on condition: £1 will buy something in relatively poor condition, but a slightly larger outlay may secure a piece in mint condition.

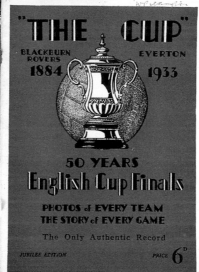

► Presented with the *Topical Times* in 1938-39, this booklet of facts and figures on players and their teams was designed to help readers predict the results of the Pools. For the collector of today it is a comprehensive "who's who" of football before 1945.

£5-10

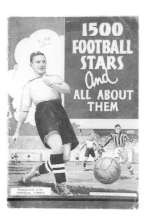

◄ These two editions of *The Cup: 50 Years of English Cup Finals* (the first edition from 1932, and the Jubilee edition from 1933), recount stories of every FA Cup final in the years 1883-1932 and 1884-1933 respectively. These books are of special interest to collectors because, in addition to the text, they include pages of contemporary advertisements for companies such as football outfitters and magazines.

£20-30 each

► The English Schools Football Association started in 1904 and now has around 14,000 affiliated schools. Published in 1954 this souvenir, traces its history, and details all aspects of this level of the game.

£5-10

◄ To celebrate the local team reaching the FA Cup Final in 1947-48, the Manchester-based *Daily Dispatch* produced this souvenir. Manchester United defeated Blackpool 4-2 in a match that is often regarded as Wembley's finest final.

£5-15

▲ Published for the 1947-48 season by *Sport – Soccer's Own Weekly Illustrated Magazine*, this souvenir includes team portraits, a gallery of goalkeepers, and club histories with comments on their chances for the coming season.

£2-5

▼ Published in 1948, this pictorial souvenir is based on *The Official History of The FA Cup* by Geoffrey Green, and describes the workings of the Challenge Cup Competition. The 1947-48 competition was won by Manchester United.

£5-10

◄ Also produced by Day & Mason (see below), these FA Cup annuals from 1951 and 1953, describe the previous year's Cup final, and preview the ongoing competition, judging the prospects of the teams who have reached the sixth round. Annuals such as these are highly prized by collectors of F.A. Cup final programmes. Newcastle United won the 1951 Cup, while Blackpool won in 1953.

£5-10 each

► In the 1950s Day & Mason Sports Annuals published a series of titles on different sports. These two football annuals contain fixture lists, action photos of well-known footballers, and highlights of the season. The cover of the 1950-51 edition features Stan Mortensen, while the 1951-52 annual shows Newcastle United's goalkeeper, Jack Fairbrother.

£5-10 each

63

Football Magazines

For many years there has been a wide range of football magazines available. The earlier soccer magazines, 1920-40, were often the sister publications of sporting papers and usually had a pools competition association, which meant that the form of football clubs was studied as closely as that of horses and jockeys – these were the popular sporting titles of the day such as *Topical Times* and *Soccer*. Other publications such as Charles Buchan's *Football Monthly*, Raich Carter's *Soccer Star*, *Goal* (which was later incorporated in *Shoot*) and *Shoot* were the popular titles of the 1950s, 1960s and 1970s, with *Shoot* surviving as a title today. The attraction of football magazines and periodicals to collectors is that even the earliest publications are usually plentiful and inexpensive, available at auctions, collectable magazine and comic dealers, jumble sales and charity shops. Collections of contemporary football magazines are fun to accumulate, and can be added to every week or month.

◄ *The Football Players Magazine: Official Journal of The Association Football Players Union*, was published monthly. This example, dated December 1923, is the first issue, and is a rare and interesting piece.

£1 each

▲ *Sport* was a very popular weekly magazine during the 1930s, 1940s and 1950s, and featured a variety of different sports. These magazines provide an interesting overview of sport in general and soccer in the context of the other popular sports.

£25 per volume

▲ In its early days *Soccer Star* bore the name of Raich Carter, one of England's finest inside-forwards of the 1930s and 1940s. It is interesting to see how the publication changed, from a newspaper to a magazine. These magazines are still quite easy to find, especially copies produced in 1950-70.

£100 for a complete set

◄ The *Topical Times*, published every Friday by D.C. Thomson & Co, was probably the most popular sports paper of its period. The weekly paper was complimented by football annuals, picture cards and souvenir booklets.

£20-40 per volume

► Organized football has been played in Malta since at least the 1920s, and in 1925-33 many British forces sides stationed in Malta contested its competitions. This Maltese edition of *Soccer Magazine*, is from June 1959.

£1 each

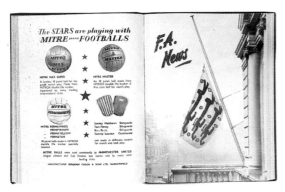

▲ The FA is the senior body of organized football and ever since its formation in 1863, the publishers of books, periodicals, magazines and other football literature have vied with each other to produce official FA titles. The *FA News* was first published as the *Football Association Bulletin* in the early 1950s and became the *FA News* for the 1956-57 season.

£80-120 for 17 volumes

◄ The *Soccer Review* was a weekly publication, popular during the 1960s, and is often found incorporated into match programmes of the period. These publications are readily available, and are inexpensive, informative and interesting to collect.

£10 per volume

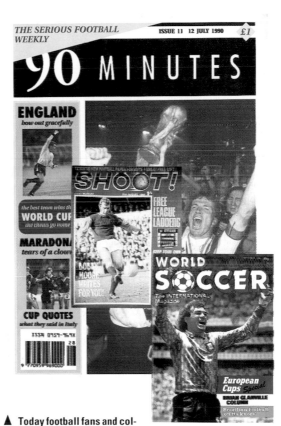

▲ Today football fans and collectors of football memorabilia are spoilt for choice by the number of soccer magazines and periodicals available every week or monthly. Three of the most popular of these are *Shoot*, *90 Minutes* and *World Soccer*. The oldest of the three, *Shoot* was first published in 1969.

£3 each

Ephemera

As the number of collecting clubs, fairs and auctions devoted to football memorabilia grows, so the range of interesting football ephemera has developed too. Collectors soon discover that, aside from match programmes, football ephemera – items of football interest of a short-lived, transitory and perishable nature – is by far the most common material available to them.

Football's collectable ephemera includes postcards, cigarette cards, photographs, autographs, and match tickets, together with some less obvious items such as postage stamps and vinyl records. Many items probably began life in the collections of football-mad schoolboys and have, by either by luck or design, survived for enthusiasts to enjoy today. Because of its very nature ephemera can be found just about anywhere, with hunting grounds such as attics, cupboards, jumble sales, charity shops and junk shops equally popular with collectors as specialist football fairs and auctions.

Many subjects included in this section, especially postcards, cigarette cards and postage stamps, have sufficient material available to develop into specialist theme collections, each with their own collecting clubs, fairs, magazines and price guides. These can make collecting more enjoyable, as they allow collectors of, say, football-related postage stamps, to meet other stamp collectors who can help and advise them on the finer points of stamp collecting in general, such as originality, reproductions, caring and storing a collection, and what and where to buy.

Cigarette cards, postcards and postage stamps are also amongst the most commonly collected ephemeral football items, possibly because they have been issued over the years with collectors in mind, and continue to be so today. Stamps have featured football since the 1920s, while overseas stamps and first day cover envelopes are regularly advertised in magazines today. Postcards, although not as popular a means of communication today as they were during the "Golden Age" of postcards, 1900-14, are still commonly available and football remains a popular subject. Cigarette cards and trade card issues have featured football related sets from the turn of the century, while the interest for card

collecting is almost as old. During the 1930s special albums were produced to contain sets of cards and this idea has been repeated more recently by other card issuers, including Brooke Bond and Panini. Collectors can gain a good idea of football's star teams and players through collecting postcards, cigarette cards and photographs, which can be built up into a "who's who" portrait gallery of footballers through the ages.

Tickets and autographs are typical of the ephemera fans obtain at football matches and are often collected along with match programmes. Throughout the history of the game men and boys have keenly sought signatures of footballers, and today these remain as collectable as examples from stage and screen actors. Autographs also have the attraction of having had the personal involvement of the signatory, especially if he or they are famous and dead – such as the Manchester United "Busby Babes" who perished at Munich during February, 1958, or other deceased football greats, such as Bobby Moore, Roy Vernon, Willie Waddell, Billy Wright, Danny Blanchflower and Sir Matt Busby. Autographs are usually found in albums or programmes, but they can also be discovered on other ordinary things, such as cigarette packets or even cheque books!

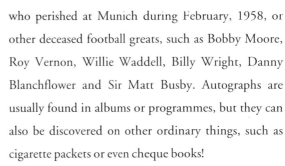

Left: A Spanish first-day cover issued for the 1982 World Cup hosted by Spain; this tournament was won by Italy. *Background image:* Detail of a group of tickets containing six Wembley Cup final tickets, including five FA Cup finals 1925-34, and one from the wartime season 1941. *Above:* A chromo-lithograph postcard of Scottish international Bobby Walker, published in Edinburgh.

Cigarette Cards 1

Cigarette cards are believed to have been first issued in Britain during the late 1880s, when football was played on muddy fields, using a heavy panelled and laced ball, by men wearing knee-length shorts and hefty boots. The first cards relating to the game of football were issued by Ogden's Ltd. of Liverpool between 1895 and

1901, amongst their extensive series of black and white photograph "Guinea Gold" General Interest subjects. A large series of Ogden's "Tabs" subjects were produced between 1900-03, which also contained a number of football cards including

many of the 12 founder-member teams of the Football League formed in 1888. Between 1910 and 1914 there was an increase in the popularity and quality of cigarette cards, usually issed in sets of 25 or 50. These cards are now fairly rare and expensive, but are rewarding to collect, and form a gallery of star players and top teams of the day. An impresive series of over 1300 cards is "Prominent Footballers" issued by Taddy & Co in 1907, 1909 and 1913. A complete set of these sepia portraits would cost around £10,500.

▶ These cards from a 1935 Scottish series issued by John Sinclair Ltd of Newcastle-upon-Tyne show photographic portraits on caricature bodies by "Boz". The players in this set are a mixture of well-known and more obscure Scottish League players from large and small clubs.

£15-20

◀ An informative series of 100 lithographic cards, showing Association Football Club Colours (1909-10). This set features action portraits of star players in the club colours of some obscure teams from England, Scotland and Ireland, such as Jas Tildesley (Leeds City), Wm Yenson (Croydon Common), C. Lynch (Derry Celtic), J. Jackson (Port Glasgow), and Andrew Aitken (Leicester Fosse). The card for Bradford City depicts E.H. Lintott (who was killed in the Somme in 1916). On the back of the card it says that the Bradford City players had "not yet distinguished themselves as cup fighters", but the team went on to win the FA Cup the following season!

£300-400

◀ A set of 50 "real photograph" cards of "English & Scottish Football Stars" (1935). Despite the title, the players in this conventional monochrome set cannot all be regarded as the stars of their period, but they do feature some international players, such as Alec James.

£20-30

◀ This 1928 50-card set by John Player & Sons also includes some rugby football players, such as Sir T.G. Devitt (Cambridge University, Blackheath and England). One notable soccer star is Warneford Cresswell, who was transferred to Sunderland in 1922 for £5,500, a record fee at the time.

£20-30

◀ F. & J. Smith (Imperial Tobacco Co (of Great Britain & Ireland Ltd), the company that issued this set of 50 club record cards for the 1920-21 season. The firm also managed to produce a similar set of cards in 1917-18 despite paper and card rationing.

£300-400

▼ Made in 1925, this set of 100 cards is a good-quality series with players from clubs as diverse as Barn, Newry and Belfast in Northern Ireland, and New Brighton and West Ham United. Card 54 features David Jack (Bolton Wanderers), who scored the first ever goal in an FA Cup final at Wembley in 1923.

£80-120

◀ These cards from a set of 110 large-size, black and white photograph cards, are approximately twice the size of standard cigarette cards, and deal with the many association football teams and rugby football teams in the Midlands region. Leading teams such as Coventry City, Port Vale, West Bromwich Albion, and Wolverhampton Wanderers, are featured alongside more obscure teams including Birmingham Corporation Tramways FC and Kenilworth Early Closers FC This set gives a very clear picture of the football world in the 1930s. The Ardath Tobacco Co who produced these cards also issued sets for Lancashire, the North-Eastern counties, Yorkshire, Scotland, and London and the Southern counties.

£80-120

◀ A supplementary set of 25 cards to "Footballers, 1928" (see above left). Issued in 1929, this series features W. Dean (Everton). It is unclear why John Player decided to wait until the second series to include Bill "Dixie" Dean – he had been scoring goals since 1923 with a regularity that has never been matched.

£15-20

Cigarette Cards 2

The 1930s are generally accepted as the heyday of cigarette cards, with large numbers of cards and sets being produced and issued by the all the major tobacco companies. Football subjects were as popular as ever before – John Player, W. D. & H. O. Wills, W. A. & A. C. Churchman and Ogden's continued to publish sets celebrating the top players and teams of the period. During this decade collecting cigarette cards became an organized hobby, with many periodicals and reference books available on the subject, and card-collecting societies appeared throughout the country.

A noteable innovation of the 1930s was the introduction of cards with adhesive backs. These "stickyback" issues were designed to be stuck down in specially produced albums. Although this seems like a good idea, sets of cards stuck in thse albums are not valued as highly as loose sets. On the other hand, the potential problem with a loose set of "stickybacks" is that if they are stored in a bundle they can become stuck to one another! The most popular way to store and present any sort of cigarette card is in a loose-leaf album with transparent leaves. This system protects the cards from discoloration and damage, and enables both the front and back of the cards to be displayed.

◄ Produced in 1935 by Ogden's Ltd., these cards of club captains have adhesive backs ("stickybacks"). Over half of this set is devoted to Rugby League, but among the soccer captains are some notable players including Alex James (Arsenal) and Arthur Rowe (Spurs).

£30-40

► Tab Cigarette cards by Ogden's Ltd, 1900–03, include many early football teams. They are fairly common as nearly 2,500 were issued.

£3-5 per card

◄ Players issued this set in 1927. It contains 50 clever caricatures by "MAC" of some great players, including amateur and professionals from England, Scotland and Wales, together with 13 Rugby Union personalities. The cards are of Players usual high standard with well researched biographies, and feature such notables of the period as W. R. ("Dixie") Dean.

£20-30

◀ These "Sporting Trophies" cards from 1927 also feature rowing, golf, rugby and boxing cups, but is one of the few sets that illustrate any football trophies. They include the Football Association Cup, Football League Championship Cup (Div. 1), and FA Amateur Cup.

£30-40

▶ This set of 50 cards from 1926 portraying apparently awkward players were an attempt by Player & Sons to give a familiar subject a new angle. Unusually, three cards depict well-known goalkeepers: Benjamin Howard Baker, Albert Iremonger, and Richard H. Pym.

£15-20

▶ Between 1922 and 1924 a series of approximately 2,463 miniature cards was issued with Pinnace Cigarettes by Godfrey Phillips Ltd. Most feature black and white portraits and measure 1¾ x 1⅓ in (45 x 35mm). The series features most first-team players from English and Scottish clubs including many sides that have since left the League or changed their names, including Aberdare Athletic, Durham City, Stalybridge Celtic and Clapton Orient.

£1,000-1,500

▼ Churchman's issued these brown and white photographic cards in September 1938, and a second series was produced for the 1939-40 season, cut short by World War 2.

£15-20

▶ Turf cigarettes were produced with these blue and white cards in 1948. They differ from pre-war issues because they were printed onto the slides inside the packets, and were designed to be cut out and mounted into albums. They give the collector an insight into football after World War 2. Indeed many of the players featured had just been demobbed and still sported military-style haircuts. The greats featured include W.E. Nicholson (Spurs), Joe Mercer (Arsenal), and Frank Swift (Manchester City).

£20-30

Trade Items

Other industries soon realised the lucrative marketing potential of presenting picture cards with their products, and were quick to follow the lead of the tobacco companies. In fact after 1900 all types of picture cards began to be issued with a wide range of products including chocolates and confectionery, ice cream and chewing gum, comics and periodicals, boys papers and magazines, newspapers, tea and coffee. Even pet food manufacturers were issuing picture cards to increase sales and encourage brand loyalty. Trade cards, however, did not tend to be produced to the same high standards as cigarette cards, and are not as collectable. Sometimes cards are poorly printed on thin card, and occasionally the text is inaccurate. The most likely reason for this inferior quality is that cigarette cards were produced for adults, while trade cards were generally aimed at a younger, less critical audience. Amongst the good sets that feature football are those issued by D. C. Thomson & Co. Ltd with the *Topical Times* sports paper during the 1930s, including the renowned "Panel Portraits" and "Star Footballers". At the end of World War 2 in 1945, the better printed trade sets were usually restricted to sports subjects, in particular the offerings of the bubble gum companies such as Chix Confectionery Co and A. & B. C. Gum (American and British Chewing Gum Ltd).

◄ "Famous Footballers" cards were produced by Barratt & Co between 1953 and 1967. The first sets were printed in black and white with portraits and facsimile signatures. This 1960 series was produced in colour, but the overall quality is lower than earlier issues.

£40-60

► Issued by A. & B.C. Gum, these large cards depict famous English League and international players from 1962-63. The reverse sides feature "Make-a-Photo" panels, which when rubbed with a coin reveal an action picture of the footballer. Some players from the 1962 World Cup in Chile are featured, such

as Jimmy Greaves (Tottenham Hotspur), Bobby Charlton (Manchester United), and Jimmy Armfield (Blackpool). The set also includes team cards for Manchester United and Everton.

£20-30

► A set of 22 cards issued with the *Adventure* boy's paper in 1923 feature black and white portraits, with signatures on the reverse. The players featured represent all three League divisions.

£20-30

▲ Issued in 1959, these cards show team colours with a nickname clue, and invite you to "Guess Which Club". Did you know West Bromwich Albion are known as "The Throstles"?

£5-10

▲ This 1969 "Football Quiz" set inlcudes coloured portraits and action photos of English and Scottish players. The backs of the cards are printed with football questions and answers – for example, card no.1 contains three questions while no.2 has the answers.

£20-30

► Produced by the Chix Confectionery Co Ltd, this is the first series of 24 cards issued with Chix and Sambo bubble gum in 1951, and feature artist-drawn illustrations. Cards in the second series contain colour photographs of leading English League players such as Jackie Milburn, Tommy Lawton, Nat Lofthouse, Alf Ramsey and Bert Trautmann. An album was available in which to keep the cards that also feature the colours of the players' teams, a career history for each footballer, and the message: "Always ask for Chix products".

£30-40

◄ This series of 48 large coloured portraits issued by A. & B. C. Gum in 1958 was the first set by this firm purely devoted to footballers. While the cards are not very well printed by today's standards they do contain well-researched biographies and football conundrums on the reverse sides. A 32-page album was available to complement the set at the cost of one shilling. Some of the players featured went on to pursue distinguished careers, including Brian Clough (Middlesborough), Bobby Charlton (Manchester United), Donald Revie (Sunderland), and Malcolm Allison (West Ham United).

£20-30

▲ Typhoo Tea Ltd issued these cards featuring International footballers in 1964. Printed on the side of the packets, they were designed to be cut out. Although basic, the set is collectable as it includes some star players of the mid-1960s, such as Gordon Banks, Derek Dougan and Roger Hunt.

£5-10

▲ These chewing gum cards from the 1968-69 season feature coloured portraits of star players from Division 1 of the Football League, with short biographies, and football quiz questions or football facts on the reverse. For example: "when was the first England v Scotland game played at Wembley?" (the answer is 1924), and: "England won the World Cup at their fifth Among the players featured are many whose clubs were enjoying success at the time, such as Eddie Gray, Rod Belfitt and Jack Charlton of Leeds United (League Champions 1968-69 season) and Tony Book, Glyn Pardoe, Mick Doyle, Tony Coleman and Mike Summerbee of Manchester City (FA Cup winners 1968-69 season).

£40-60

▼ A set of 16 booklets was issued by Esso in 1971 and were given away to customers with purchases of petrol. These small booklets ("known as Squelchers!") contain pages of football facts and coloured illustrations, and were intended to "squelch" or settle football arguments. Collectors were encouraged to "Be a Champion Squelcher. Collect all 16 Books in the series." The set includes the following titles, "Goalkeeping Greats", "The World Cup Story", "Club Colours and Nicknames", "Language of Football", "Star Strikers", "Masters of Defence", "League Champs", "England", "Scotland", "Wales" and "Northern Ireland". The inside back cover of each booklet features a cartoon of a red-faced man and the legend "I've been squelched!"

£15-30

▼ The Esso FA Cup Centenary Medals 1872-1972 collection comprises 31 medals that were presented free with petrol purchases during 1972. The set includes one gold-coloured medal with the crest of the English FA, and details of the 1972 winners (Leeds United), and 30 silver-coloured medals bearing the crests of previous winning teams.

£30-40

▲ *The Rover Handy Album of Famous Football Jerseys*, and *Pocket Guide to Football Club Colours*, were presented free with *The Rover*. These colourful booklets measuring 5¾ x 4⅜ in (14.5 x 11.1cm) were not collected quite as keenly as the cards, and as a consequence they are quite rare today. The two examples shown here are in unusually good condition.

£20-40

NOEL CANTWELL

ALEX FORBES

JOHN HOLLOWBREAD   JACK McGUGAN

NAT LOFTHOUSE

MALCOLM ALLISON

◀ Presented with *Adventure* boy's paper in 1957, this set of cards features many top international players from the English and Scottish Leagues. Sadly, one of the players included, Duncan Edwards was soon to die from injuries sustained in the Manchester United air crash at Munich on 6 February 1958.

£40-60

▼ This 1970 Esso World Cup coin collection was described at the time as "a collector's item, never to be re-issued … a valuable souvenir of a milestone in soccer history – the World Cup 1970". Each of the 30 silver-coloured coins bears a portrait and autograph of members of England's 1970 World Cup squad.

£30-40

▲ These varnished black and white portrait cards were issued by D. C. Thomson and presented with the *Wizard* in 1959. This set of "Football Stars" cards was produced as a companion to "World Cup Footballers", a series that was issued jointly in 1958 by the *Adventure, Hotspur, Rover* and *Wizard* boy's magazines. Despite the title, the personalities featured on these cards are a mixture of stars featured alongside players that have been almost forgotten! Card 30 shows Noel Cantwell, then the captain of West Ham United, and an Irish international.

£40-60

◀ This sleeve contains metal disc portraits of "22 Soccer Superstars" that were issued by Esso during 1974. The players featured in this fantasy Great Britain football team are from England, Scotland, Northern Ireland and Wales, and comprise Colin Bell, Billy Bremner, Martin Chivers, Kenny Dalglish, Mike England, Eddie Gray, David Hay, Emlyn Hughes, Norman Hunter, Leighton James, Pat Jennings, Kevin Keegan, Peter Lorimer, Malcolm Macdonald, Paul Madeley, Rodney Marsh, Roy McFarland, Bobby Moore, Martin Peters, Peter Shilton, Peter Storey and John Toshack.

£20-30

Postcards 1

Amongst the merchandize available to fans at most football club supporters shops today, there is usually a wide array of colourful postcards picturing the teams and portraits of star players. Cards such as these have been popular with fans since the Edwardian era, and are now eagerly sought after by collectors of postcards and football memorabilia alike. The majority of valuable football postcards were published during what is now referred to as the "Golden Age" of postcards, 1900-14. During these years

Britain was deluged by a flood of pictorial cards. They were decorative and inexpensive, while postage cost merely half an old penny for a same-day postal service! These cards offer the collector the opportunity to accumulate an interesting and relatively inexpensive pictorial history of football throughout the 20th century.

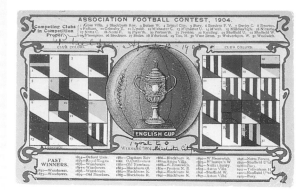

▲ Produced before the final of the 1903-04 FA Cup Competition, this card features the names and colours of 32 competing clubs. Manchester City won their first FA Cup by beating Bolton Wanderers, of Division 2, by 1-0.

£40-60

◀ Featuring the members of Woolwich Arsenal FC (changed to Arsenal FC in 1913) in 1907-08, this card would be popular with collectors of Arsenal memorabilia, as well as with people who specialize in teams that have changed their name or ceased to exist.

£40-60

▼ Published locally in Birmingham around 1905, this charming colour-tinted card shows the main covered stand at Aston Villa's Villa Park, Trinity Road. The club moved to Villa Park in 1897, having previously played at Aston Park, 1874-76 and Perry Barr 1876-97.

£40-60

Tower Entrance
Stadium, Wembley.

◄ This postcard, showing the Tower Entrance at Wembley Stadium during the mid-1920s was produced by Raphael Tuck, who made a huge amount of postcards during the first half of this century. His most collectable football-related sets feature football teams and players in the early 1900s, and are entitled, "Celebrated Association Football Clubs", "Celebrated Football Players" and "Famous Football Players". Each series contains six cards and complete sets are quite rare.

£20-30

▲ These identical cards were published to celebrate Wolverhampton Wanderers reaching (left), and then winning (right), the FA Cup final against Newcastle United in 1908. Wolves won 3-1.

£30-40 each

▼ This attractive card, was produced in April 1926 to celebrate Bolton Wanderers' second FA Cup final in three years. The slogan mimics the radio call signal of the BBC.

£40-60

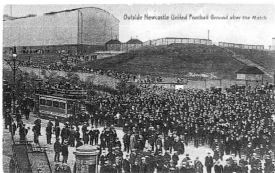

Outside Newcastle United Football Ground after the Match

▲ Published in 1910, this card "Outside Newcastle United Football Ground After the Match", is an evocative picture of football in the north of England before World War 1. At this time "The Magpies" were an extremely successful side.

£30-40

Postcards 2

Postcards, after stamps, are the second most commonly collected item in Great Britain, and cartology – postcard collecting – has become a serious hobby. Collectors of football postcards have a huge range of subjects to choose from to create specialized or general collections, and they are also fortunate that many postcard fairs and collecting clubs exist to cater for their interest. The more interesting collections, some of which have been put on public exhibition, have concentrated exclusively on portraits of players, English and Scottish football grounds and stadia, football humour, and team portraits. These are amongst the most common football postcard themes and so are the easiest to build into collections of any substance. Generally speaking, collectors of football memorabilia soon learn not to purchase the first thing offered to them and this is certainly true in the case of football postcards. By and large football postcards are not terribly rare and around £30 usually buys an interesting old example in good condition, with sharp, unworn corners, and a surface free from stains or creases. Postcards which have been autographed by footballers are considered a bonus and, contrary to popular belief, cards that have been written on and posted are not worth less than unused examples, and can sometimes carry interesting comments on past footballing events.

▲ This pair of German postcards was published in Berlin as souvenirs of the Germany v England International match at the Olympic Stadium, Berlin on 14 May 1938. Only issued in Germany these cards are rare. The England card is made more collectable because it has been autographed by the team.

£150-200

▲ Football is also featured on the colourful, vulgar, but humorous postcards typical of the 1950s and 1960s, such as the one seen here.

£5-40

▲ Frank Swift of Manchester City and England, one of the game's finest and most popular goal-keepers, has autographed this portrait postcard making it a collectable piece.

£40-60

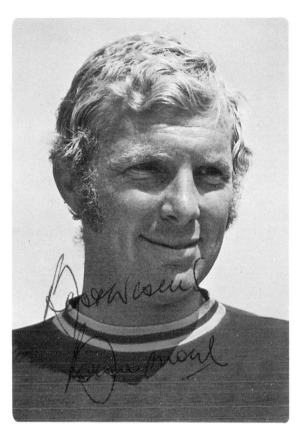

◀ Typical of the types of postcards available to football enthusiasts at football club shops, the autograph on this colour portrait card of Bobby Moore makes it much more collectable. Captain of West Ham United, England's most capped outfield player (he received 108 caps), and one of the finest centre-backs in the game's history, Moore sadly died in February 1993, aged 51. He was elected Footballer of the Year in 1964, and in 1974 he was awarded the OBE.

£40-60 with autograph £5-10 postcard only

▲ Non-British cards, such as this promotional item for the 1958 World Cup held in Sweden, are relatively uncommon and are of particular interest to many collectors. This card features the flags of the 16 qualifying teams.

£30-40

▲ Geoff Hurst, featured here on this autographed action portrait postcard, is probably most famous for scoring the first-ever hat-trick in a World Cup final, when he helped England defeat West Germany 4-2 after extra time at Wembley on 30 July 1966. A West Ham United player, Hurst also won 49 caps and scored 24 international goals for England between 1966 and 1972.

£20-30

▲ A very interesting piece, this 1966 souvenir postcard featuring the England mascot "World Cup Willie" has been autographed by Geoff Hurst (see left), and also features the first day cover of the World Cup 1966 stamp that was over-printed "England Winners". Issued on 18 August, the stamp was limited to 12 million copies and most Post Offices had completely sold out within a few hours.

£40-60

Autographs 1

The majority of autographs are found within the pages of albums designed to be compact enough to fit into a trouser pocket. Most football autograph collections date from the 1930s and 1950s, when British football enjoyed its spectator booms, and were usually collected by football-crazy, football-mad schoolboys! However, autographs are more desirable on photographs or other official printed matter concerning the players or teams such as programmes, books, menus or even football equipment. In the same way as collectors of cricketana prize cricket bats that have been signed by famous players or touring teams, so collectors of football memorabilia are frequently on the look-out for autographed footballs or signed shirts. Many items in this category often claim to be the actual equipment or kit used in certain matches by individuals or teams on specific occasions. When purchasing items such as these, or any autographs of rarity and high value, is always advisable to enquire about their provenance. The dealer or auctioneer should know where the autographs came from, and whether or not they are likely to be genuine. It is also useful to obtain a photocopy or photograph of an authentic signature for comparison when hunting for particular autographs. This precaution can help to identify forgeries and avoid disappointment.

◀ Two pages from a typical album of autographs collected during the 1930s, which also includes signatures from cricketers, speedway riders and film stars. The album is well presented with small portraits of the sportsmen or stars gummed beside the featured signature/signatures. Unfortunately, today albums like this are usually broken-up and sold to specialist collectors.

£80-120

▲ Two pages of autographs signed at a dinner given by Arsenal FC and Huddersfield Town at the Hotel Great Central on the evening of 26 April 1930, to celebrate the FA Cup Final won by Arsenal 2-0. These autographs are good clear examples, and include the signatures of James and Lambert, Arsenal's goal scorers on the day.

£150-200

▼ Collected following a wartime international match, England v Scotland, played at Wembley on 10 October 1942, these rather creased autograph pages bear 24 signatures from the two sides, including Stanley Matthews, Bill Shankly and Matt Busby. Unfortunately, the ink has faded, and the poor condition of the programme will reduce the value of the autographs.

£20-40

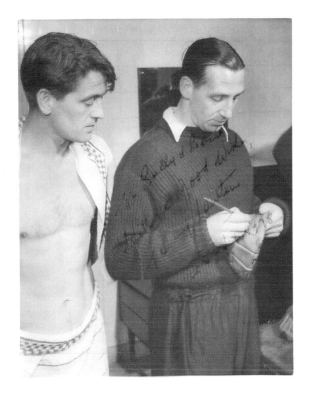

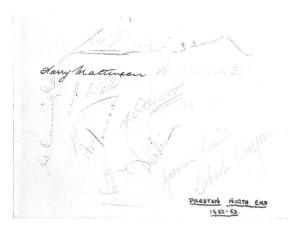

◀ An autographed photo-
graph of the great Tommy
Lawton, showing him sign-
ing footballs for fans after a
training session.

£30-60

▲ A team portrait of
Chelsea FC, League Cham-
pions for the 1954-55 season, with 12 ink signatures
on the surrounding mount.

£100-150

▲ An interesting piece, this wartime international programme, Scotland v England, played on 18 April 1942, has been
autographed by the Scottish team. While collectable, it would
be worth more if it were in better condition.

£40-70

▲ This page, featuring the signatures of Preston North End
1952-53, is taken from an album of autographs that has had its
contents individually mounted on cards. It is typical of many
football autographs available through specialist dealers.

£20-40

Autographs 2

Autographs are amongst the most widely collected areas of football memorabilia – a fact that was as true 50 years ago as it is today. And remember that the collections of today will become the collectable items of tomorrow! There are many ways of collecting football autographs. The most enjoyable way to acquire the autographs of modern footballers is to collect them in person. This can be achieved in a number of ways. The favourite method with many fans is to wait patiently outside football grounds or training grounds in the hope of meeting the players and getting their signatures. Other fans and collectors simply send their albums to clubs or fan clubs requesting autographs. Another way of obtaining autographs is to attend charity events hosted by football clubs or the opening of sports shops – both events often feature football stars to attract the attention of the general public and local publicity. Many collectors of modern football autographs travel everywhere with their books and photographs of favourite players … just in case! For many active fans of football, autograph hunting is as much a part of the game as collecting programmes and, of course, attending the matches.

▲ Two pages from an autograph album containing signatures of eleven of the ill-fated Manchester United team of 1957-58. The autographs were obtained by David Pegg just before the Munich air disaster of 6 February 1958. These autographs are very collectable.

£400-600

▲ This page from a typical schoolboy's autograph album of the period, contains signatures of the League Division 1 Championship-winning Arsenal team from the 1952-53 season, and features many international stars, and players that went on to become managers.

£80-120

◀ In 1961, an English FA team known as "Tom Finney's 1961 team" went on tour to the Far East and New Zealand. Although relatively recent, this collection is unusual because such tours are now rare.

£40-70

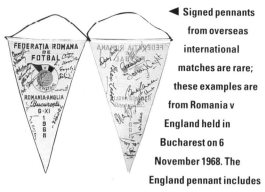

◀ Signed pennants from overseas international matches are rare; these examples are from Romania v England held in Bucharest on 6 November 1968. The England pennant includes Alf Ramsey (Manager), Bobby Moore (West Ham United), Gordon West (Everton), Tommy Wright (Everton), Alan Ball (Everton), Roger Hunt (Liverpool), Martin Peters (West Ham United), Bobby Charlton (Manchester United) and Alan Mullery (Tottenham Hotspur). Unfortunately, all the autographs, except that of Sir Alf Ramsey, have been signed using a felt tip pen which has smudged, but they are still collectable.

£50-80 for two pennants

▼ Two pages from an impressive album containing a good collection of English and Scottish Football League team autographs from 1970-71 season, including national teams from each of the four home countries (Scotland and England are seen here). The album features players' signatures from a total

of 129 clubs. Collections as comprehensive as this are difficult to assemble and therefore quite rare. In this case individual pages from the album were sent to every League club in England Wales and Scotland. Not all were returned complete, but some even included the autographs of the groundsmen and team physiotherapist.

£300-500

▲ A centre-page autograph sheet from an entrance programme for Ted Ditchburn's Testimonial Match between the Internationals Club and Spurs 1950 at Brooklands, Romford on 14 March 1965. Three then-current Spurs players officiated on the day: Dave MacKay as referee, and Jimmy Greaves and Terry Dyson as linesmen. The Internationals Club was formed from international players of all four home countries to play charity matches in Britain and abroad.

£20-40

▲ In the early 1970s under the management of Bill Nicholson, Tottenham Hotspur were enjoying considerable success. The 1970-71 squad, seen here in an autographed photo, won the League Cup that season. Spurs won the League Cup again in 1972-73, and between times they won the UEFA Cup in 1971-72.

£20-40

Photographs

By the time the Football Association was formed at the Freemason's Tavern in Holborn, London during 1863, photography was already a relatively common, though expensive, form of record and portraiture. Because many of these 19th and early 20th century football photographs have survived, collectors and enthusiasts can gain an insight into the game during its early years. The earliest known "action" photograph of an association football match features the 1887 Cup final between Aston Villa and their local rivals West Bromwich Albion. The picture captures Albion forward Bayliss heading for goal in front of 15,000 spectators at the Oval, and shows players wearing external shin pads, goals without nets (not introduced until 1891) and the goalkeeper wearing the same strip as his team-mates. The majority of antique and collectable football photographs tend to be team portraits, and portraits of specific players of fame or importance. Many are found in scrapbooks, amongst newspaper cuttings, football programmes and ephemera. Photographs of League clubs and international teams are the most sought-after and the most valuable, while equally interesting portraits of Victorian and Edwardian church teams and factory teams are usually more affordable.

▲ Third Lanark FC, one of the eleven founder members of the Scottish League, were based in Glasgow and were one of the leading sides during the early history of Scottish football. This photograph celebrates their victory in the Glasgow Charity Cup, 1890.

£100-150

▼ A sepia-tinted photograph of Heart of Midlothian football team (named after a novel by Sir Walter Scott), winners of the Scottish Cup 1890-91. This piece has been mounted on card.

£80-120

▲ This autographed portrait photograph features Charlie Roberts, the finest centre-half of his time. Beginning his career with Darlington, Roberts moved to Grimsby and then to Manchester United in 1904.

£100-150

TORONTO ASSOCIATION FOOT-BALL CLUB.

▲ A rare piece, this black and white team portrait photograph features a Canadian team, the Toronto Association Foot-Ball Club, 1884. The first game of football in Canada to be played according to British Football Association rules, was in 1876.

£300-400

RANGERS F.C. WINNERS OF THE GLASGOW CUP SCOTTISH CUP AND CHARITY CUP 1896-97

▲ By the end of the 1896-97 season, Rangers FC had won the Glasgow Cup, the Scottish Cup and the Charity Cup, and the players are seen here together with their trophies. Rangers enjoyed a great deal of success at the end of the 19th century.

£100-150

▼ The value of this photograph featuring the 1935-36 FA Cup winners Arsenal, is enhanced because it features the players' autographs. Arsenal dominated soccer in the 1930s, and in the 1936 Cup Final on 25 April, beat Sheffield United 1-0 with a goal by Ted Drake in the 74th minute.

£300-400

▼ During the first decade of the 20th century Newcastle United was the strongest football team in England. Between 1905 and 1910 they were League Champions three times, and FA Cup finalists five times (although they won the Cup only once, in 1910). This team portrait was taken for the 1909-10 season.

£100-150

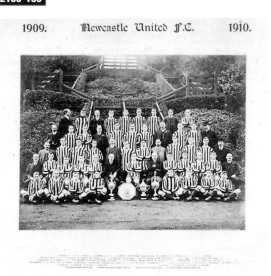

1909.　Newcastle United F.C.　1910.

Football Match Tickets

Football match tickets, which can vary enormously in size, colour and design, are not an obvious area of collectable football ephemera. But many fans collect tickets alongside football programmes, and as such tickets can enhance the programme's appeal and contribute to the comprehensiveness of a collection. Like other examples of football ephemera, the condition of tickets is very important to their value and desirability. For example, most tickets available to collectors are the "used" stubs returned to spectators. These are therefore incomplete tickets - and yet surprisingly unused tickets for internationals, Cup matches or finals are sometimes discovered in perfect condition. Obviously, such tickets are very rare and, depending on the match, more valuable. Football match tickets do present collectors with a reasonably inexpensive area of collecting, but it is important to remember that reproductions and forgeries do exist. For many years now forgers have produced fake tickets to sell to unwary fans who have been unable to obtain tickets through the usual official channels. Collectors should be as aware of these forgeries as fans need to be.

▲ Between 1872 and 1900, British international matches were confined to teams within the British Isles. This ticket for England v Scotland at Blackburn, on 4 April 1891, was the 20th meeting of the two countries and resulted in a 2-1 victory for England. Tickets of this age are quite rare. This example is torn, and its value is correspondingly reduced.

£20-40

▼ The 1924 FA Cup final was played between Newcastle United and Aston Villa on 26 April. This ticket is larger than today's Cup final tickets, and bears the Wembley Lion which was chosen as the symbol for the Empire Exhibition held in 1924.

£20-40

▲ In spite of the mounting tension in Europe, France was chosen to stage the 1938 World Cup. The competition still attracted 36 entries, with 16 qualifying for the finals. This ticket, priced 20 francs, is from the quarter-final between France and Italy,

£20-40

▼ Tottenham Hotspur became the first team this century to achieve the Football League Championship and FA Cup double in 1961. This "double-winning" ticket is of particular interest to collectors.

£5-10

▲ A rare and collectable piece, this ticket was produced for the second leg of the 1957-58 European Cup quarter-final, between Manchester United and Red Star Belgrade held in Yugoslavia on 5 February 1958. The "Busby Babes" returned home in high spirits having secured a draw that guaranteed them a place in the semi-final. But tragically, the plane that was carrying them crashed, killing among others players, team staff, and journalists.

£50-100

▼ Before the 1970 World Cup, it was decided that If Italy, Uruguay or Brazil, who had each won the Jules Rimet Trophy on two previous occasions, won again, they would be presented with the trophy outright. This ticket is from the opening game of the finals on 31 May, in which Mexico and Russia achieved only a goalless draw. The 1970 competition ended with the trophy becoming the permanent property of Brazil.

£5-10

▲ During the Coronation year, 1953, English football fans were shaken by the team's first home defeat by a Continental side. On 25 November, England were beaten 6-3 by Hungary at Wembley. The Hungarian victory was achieved by goals from Hidegkuti (3), Puskas (2) and Bozsik. Sewell, Mortensen and Ramsey all scored for England.

£10-15

▼ This World Cup '94 USA ticket, priced at $180, was issued for the final match contested between Brazil and Italy and played at the Rose Bowl in Los Angeles, on 17 July 1994. The Brazilian side won the competition following a penalty shoot-out after extra time. This was the first competition to be decided by a shoot-out, although the 1990 competition between West Germany and Argentina was decided by a single penalty. Little more than a momento at present, this ticket may become more collectable in the future.

£2-5

Football Postage Stamps

For many years now collecting stamps has been the most popular hobby in Great Britain and Europe. The appeal is that stamps are universally available, small, colourful, decorative and relatively inexpensive. There is also the added advantage of a great deal of associated literature and specialist dealers. More and more frequently special issues are produced to commemorate special events such as big sporting events or, in this case, the game of Association Football. In addition to stamps, collectors of football memorabilia may find themselves drawn to the many decorative and colourful first day covers. The fashion for collecting these stamps, used on complete envelopes on the first day of their issue, has grown in many countries during the last 30 years or so, with the result that earlier examples have become much sought after. It is certainly true that particular stamp subjects are more collectable and valuable than others, sport and football in particular. However it is fortunate that the number of countries producing football related stamps is growing, as the game becomes ever more popular around the world.

▶ In 1924, Uruguay won the Olympic Games soccer tournament in Paris, and these stamps were issued to commemorate the occasion. After the 1926 FIFA Congress, it was declared that the Olympic Games no longer represented the world's best football, and two years later FIFA decided to hold the World Cup every four years.

£40-60

▲ Produced in Chile, this first day cover features four 1962 World Cup stamps featuring images of South American football, and views of Santiago football stadium – one of several new stadia built for the competition. This item is dated 30 May 1962, the date of the opening matches.

£40-60

▼ In their first home defeat by a Continental side, England were beaten 6-3 by Hungary at Wembley on 25 November 1953. Previously unknown Hungarian players, such as Puskas, Kocsis and Bosnik, soon became household names in England. Back in Hungary, the team were honoured with a commemorative stamp.

£30-40

▲ In 1981, Monaco issued this stamp to commemorate the 25th anniversary of the European Champion Clubs' Cup, better known as the European Cup. The 25th European Cup was won by Liverpool, who defeated Real Madrid 1-0 on 29 May 1981. This stamp was issued specially for collectors.

£2-5

► Issued to celebrate West Germany's World Cup success, this illustrated first day cover, dated 7 July 1974, features a team portrait of the victorious side. The 1974 World Cup, hosted by West Germany, was a larger competition with a new trophy.

£10-20

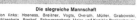

◄ Featuring stamps from France, Brazil and Sweden, this postcard was made for the 1966 British National Stamp Exhibition, during which the Jules Rimet trophy was stolen.

£10-20

▼ Issued for the World Cup USA 1994, this first day cover reflects some of the razzle-dazzle of the North American event. This example, post-marked Orlando, Florida, and dated 26 May 1994, lists the 24 teams involved in the tournament and illustrates the nine venues where the six groups played their matches.

£2-5

▲ Printed in three languages, this first day cover was issued in Argentina to commemorate the opening matches of the 1978 World Cup finals. Argentina won the Cup for the first time when they beat the Netherlands 3-1 after extra time, in the River Plate Stadium in Buenos Aires on 25 June 1978. Scotland was the only representative from the British Isles in this year, but did not make it into the second stage.

£10-15

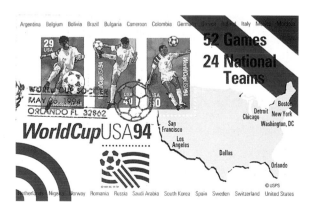

1966 World Cup 1

It is surprising how few good quality souvenirs and collectables there are from the 1966 World Cup finals. Most items available to collectors of football memorabilia are either publications such as programmes, newspapers, magazines and countless books, or items of ephemera including World Cup final tickets, autographs and rosettes. World Cup Willie, the cheeky little "Lionhearted" mascot of the England team – who was first introduced to the English football public in *Soccer Review* during August 1965 – was reproduced as inexpensive souvenir figures, car-mascots, tea-towels and pin-badges, as well as appearing on packaging of World Cup products. "Willie Football", a game described at the time as "a sparkling World Cup souvenir", was based on the old table top game played with two pennies and a halfpenny, while Gordon Banks (the England goalkeeper) and Derek Dougan (Irish international centre-forward) were photographed actually playing it! In general these souvenirs remain available to collectors today and, because they were not made to a very high quality, they are relatively inexpensive.

◄ This special souvenir early edition of the *Evening Standard* of 30 July 1966, declares that England "will be Champions". It contains photographs, a soccer quiz and team portraits. It is not in very good condition, being both creased and slightly torn, and so the value is correspondingly low.

£15-30

◄ Published by Beaverbrook Newspapers Ltd this 48-page booklet is a sports person's delight. The World Cup is reported from day one with England v Uruguay, all the way through to "the moment England grasped the fact that the World Cup was won". The remaining contents include reports on the main boxing, cricket, tennis, horse racing and domestic football events of the year.

£15-30

◄ The *Radio Times* from 9-15 July 1966 devoted 12 pages to the tournament. It includes a programme of matches together with profiles of television and radio commentators. It is an interesting souvenir, and is quite rare today.

£30-50

▲ London Transport and British Railways produced this travel guide on how to get to London's Wembley and White City Stadia by bus, train and underground. Although rare, this piece has no real value.

£1-2

▼ This FA programme was printed for the final match held on 30 July 1966. This particular piece is rapidly increasing in value, and a number of forgeries are known to exist. However, it is an essential part of any collection and contains results and action photographs from the group matches, together with team details and portraits of the finalists.

£30-50

▲ Produced by the FA, the official souvenir programme shown here, was available throughout England and covered all the World Cup matches including the final. Printed in four languages: English, French, German and Spanish, it contains portraits of the participating teams, details of the tournament referees and advertisements for a number of World Cup products.

◄ A rare and unusual piece, this handbook, issued by the BBC and ITV, was designed for use by visiting television broadcasters covering the World Cup.

£40-60

£30-50

◄ The 1966 World Cup competition spawned many souvenirs, such as this cigar box, and "World Cup Willie" the official England team mascot, appeared on many products between 1965 and 1970. Much of the money earned by Willie went towards subsidizing the 1966 World Cup and supporting the England team. Other 1966 World Cup products included Watney's World Cup Ale, Tudor World Cup Crisps and G.F. Lovell's "World Cup Willie" sweets. Surviving examples of packaging such as this are rare, simply because they were not produced for very long, and most were thrown away. Although interesting for the collector, this cigar box does not possess any intrinsic value.

£1-2

1966 World Cup 2

1966 is the only occasion that England have ever won the World Cup, and nearly 30 years later fans of English football still talk about it! For collectors today there is a wide variety of items available from this period, but be wary as quality is not always good. World Cup souvenirs available to fans at the time included wall pennants, key-rings, wall shields, footballs, England football player figures, travelling bags, shoulder bags and medallions, all decorated with the Jules Rimet Cup insignia and World Cup Willie, or inscribed "World Cup 1966". Fortunately, collectors of football memorabilia occasionally stumble upon more interesting and unusual souvenirs or items from the 1966 World Cup - such as shirts worn by the players of competing teams, footballs signed by the victorious England team, official FA flags and badges, and rarely, World Cup medals awarded to the teams and officials.

▼ England issued three stamps on 1 June 1966 to commemorate the 1966 World Cup – the first British stamps to feature sportsmen in action. This collectable envelope bears the official World Cup final postmark for 30 July 1966, and also bears eleven autographs of England's World Cup winning squad.

£80-120

▼ Produced by popular home-movie makers Walton Films, this official World Cup final 8mm film with sound, features all the highlights of England's nerve-racking and thrilling match in which they beat West Germany 4-2 to become the World Champions.

£15-30

◄ This figure of mascot World Cup Willie is typical of the souvenirs available to fans and collectors throughout 1965 and 1966. World Cup Willie, wearing a sombrero on his head, was England's mascot again for the 1970 World Cup in Mexico.

£40-60

◄ Amongst the souvenirs produced to commemorate the 1966 World Cup were diecast gilt metal replicas of the Jules Rimet trophy (8in, 20.3cm high). This example was one of many presented to officials of the FA during victory banquets held in honour of the England victory.

£500-800

▼ This World Cup special commemorative issue First Day Cover features the popular 4d 1966 World Cup stamp overprinted "England Winners", together with the important "Harrow and Wembley" postmark. These covers were limited to 12 million copies, but the demand was so great that most Post Offices sold out in hours. This example has been written on, and is therefore less valuable than a similar piece in pristine condition.

£40-60

▲ Corner flags such as this one were used at the eight grounds where the 1966 World Cup matches were played: Wembley Stadium, White City, Middlesbrough, Sheffield Wednesday, Manchester United, Aston Villa, Everton and Sunderland. Whilst the FA commissioned many official flags and cornerflags for the World Cup tournament, they are nevertheless quite rare today and very collectable.

£300-500

▼ Breweries in Britain traditionally produce commemorative beers and ales for special occasions, usually Royal events such as coronations and weddings. Watney Mann, famous for their beers and brown ales, brewed a special Pale Ale and christened it "World Cup Ale". In addition to the ale, which was widely advertised in football programmes and magazines, Watney Mann also produced special commemorative beer mats, drinking glasses and promotional pennants.

World Cup Ale, unopened £10, opened £2-5 Beer Mat £1-3 Ale Glass £5-10 Pennant £20-30

▲ Liverpool's Roger Hunt played a vital role in England's World Cup success; he played in all six England games, scoring three goals. This red no. 21 jersey was worn by Hunt in the final. Such pieces are very rare and extremely collectable.

£1,000-2,000

Other World Cups

The FIFA World Cup competition enjoys a special place in the hearts of football enthusiasts, and therefore memorabilia from the various tournaments are amongst the most sought-after of football collectables. It is the competition that all national representative teams want to win, and as it has grown in both size and popularity, so the amount of official and unofficial literature, programmes, souvenirs, collectables and ephemera has increased. World Cup USA '94 was an extremely profitable venture, and with the huge amount of sponsorship (including Coca-Cola and Canon), merchandise (a cartoon dog called "Striker" created by Warner Bros was the official mascot) and global TV rights, was almost as much about big business as it was about international football. However, there are now many souvenirs for collectors to seek and acquire. Compared to the total of 13 nations that participated in the first World Cup competition in Uruguay in 1930, the 1994 World Cup finals comprised 24 countries from among the original 143 entries.

▼ Published in 1958, this book is a good and informative, round-by-round, eye-witness account of the sixth World Cup competition, staged in Sweden during the summer of 1958. Author John Camkin was a respected football journalist with the *News Chronicle*, where he had served his apprenticeship under Charlie Buchan, at one time one of the game's finest inside forwards, and later one of Fleet Street's most distinguished football correspondents.

£10-20

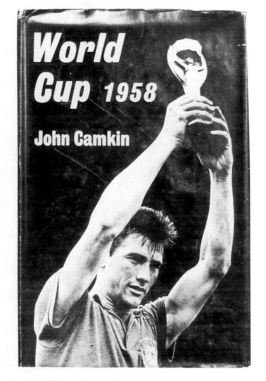

▼ This old leather suitcase once belonged to an official from the FA/FIFA between the 1950s and 1960s. From the various labels it is clear that he travelled widely, including Chile for the 1962 World Cup where England reached the quarter-finals, and also to Italy for the 1966-68 European Championship semi-finals, where England lost 1-0 to Yugoslavia in Florence. England went on to defeat the USSR 2-0 in the match for third place.

£30-40

▼ Produced for the 1954 World Cup in Switzerland, this programmes, which features the design used on all programmes issued for the competition, is from one of England's three Group 4 games against Belgium, Switzerland and Italy. England reached the quarter-finals where they lost 4-2 to Uruguay. The final was eventually contested by West Germany and Hungary, at Berne on 4 July 1954, with the German team recovering from 0-2 to win 3-2.

£30-40 each

▼ Published in 1978, this is a good and comprehensive account of the eleventh World Cup which was hosted by Argentina. Scotland, the only representative from the British Isles, finished third in their group. The book reports on the successes of Argentina, Holland and Italy, and concentrates on the downfall of the West German team, and the disappointment of the Scottish squad.

£15-30

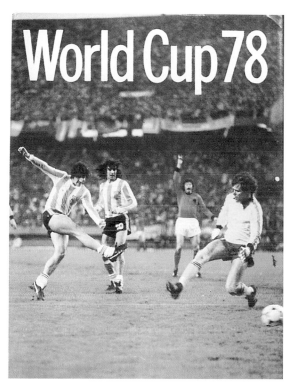

▲ The World Cup final tournaments from 1966 have each been represented by a mascot. Sometimes, too, individual competing countries have mascots. In 1982 England's mascot was "Bulldog Bobby", while Spain used a smiling orange called "Naranjito". The character above, "Juanito", was used to represent the 1970 Mexico World Cup.

£40-60

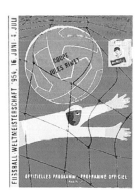

▶ Written by Donald Saunders of *The Daily Telegraph*, this book presents a full and graphic account of the 1962 World Cup. This example is in good condition complete with its decorative dust wrapper.

£5-10

▶ Special bottles of Italian white wine were produced for the 1990 World Cup, hosted by Italy. Similar commemorative bottles of red and white wines were produced in Spain for World Cup USA '94, with bottles in the shape of footballs, players and trophies. These bottles are collectable especially if unopened and complete with contents.

£10-20

Football Records

Prior to the almost universal availability of video tapes and video recorders today, the ultimate "recorded" football souvenir available to fans and collectors were therecordings to celebrate football events produced by specialist record companies during the 1960s, 1970s and 1980s. These records, which also include a number of popular club songs that enjoyed moderate success in the record charts, were released either in advance of, or later as souvenirs of, celebrated football matches. Games such as this include domestic and European competition finals or international matches – and were designed to be mementoes in sound for the fans to treasure, to help them to recall memorable moments for a long time afterwards. Football recordings such as these are easily affordable and are commonly available in second-hand record shops. Collectors should only consider good examples which are unscratched and complete with their album sleeves and any associated posters or literature.

▲ In the 1971 FA Cup final between Arsenal and Liverpool, Arsenal were "gunning" for the League and Cup double. In an exciting period of extra time after a goal-less first 90 minutes, Arsenal won 2-1.

£10-15

▲ This souvenir album, "Salute To Stoke! – 1972 Football League Cup Final" was to celebrate the team's first major trophy in 109 years, following their surprise win over Chelsea. The record features match highlights recorded at Wembley.

£10-15

▼ A 33⅓ rpm recording was made of the 1968 European Cup final between Manchester United and Benfica at Wembley on 29 May 1968. It features highlights of the first and second halves and extra time, and was released by arrangement with BBC Radio Enterprises, with Alan Clarke and Peter Jones as commentators. Manchester United won 4-1.

£20-30

◀ The Milk Cup officially came into being on 1 March 1982 when the Football League Cup was renamed on its sponsorship by the National Dairy Council. Other sponsors for this trophy have followed, including Littlewoods and Coca-Cola. The 1984 Milk Cup was a Merseyside derby, Liverpool v Everton. This recording charts the events of the "Friendly Final". Following a 0-0 draw on 25 March, the replay was held on 28 March. Liverpool won with a single goal by Graeme Souness.

£5-10

▲ The 1971 European Cup Winners Cup final between Chelsea and Real Madrid was played in Athens on 19 May 1971. The first game ended in a 1-1 draw, though goalkeeper Peter Bonetti had to keep Real Madrid at bay throughout extra time to ensure a replay. On 21 May, Chelsea fought hard to win 2-1. The cover of this souvenir recording shows the victorious Chelsea captain, Ron "Chopper" Harris, holding the European Cup Winners Cup surrounded by team-mates.

£10-20

▲ Released in 1981, this collection of commentaries and club songs celebrates 100 years of the FA Cup, featuring songs that have been adopted by particular clubs, such as Spurs' *Nice One Cyril* (dedicated to Cyril Knowles), and West Ham's *I'm Forever Blowing Bubbles*, and of course, *You'll Never Walk Alone*.

£5-10

▶ Released by Pye Records in 1970 prior to the World Cup finals in Mexico, "The World Beaters Sing The World Beaters" by the 1970 England Football Squad, contains a colourful 10-page football-shaped album sleeve showing scenes from the 1966 World Cup final between England and West Germany.

£20-30

Miscellaneous Ephemera 1

Football has been an important part of British life for over a century. In that long period the game has spawned a large and diverse selection of miscellaneous objects and items: souvenir footballs, commemorative football programmes, tobacco pipes carved with footballs and the like. And as the game spread throughout Europe and the Americas during the late 19th century, and subsequently developed into a global sport, the amount and choice of football memorabilia has grown. Who would ever have guessed that late 20th century phone-cards would be decorated with portraits of footballers and football teams! Today football memorabilia is still growing and becoming more plentiful. One reason for this is that the game is a large commercial business, and merchandise is now a very important source of a top clubs' revenue. Supporters' shops are usually crammed full of a rich miscellany of new souvenirs and memorabilia for the collector. Some young collectors are already purchasing 1994-95 season memorabilia safe in the knowledge that one day it will be old and interesting ... and maybe valuable.

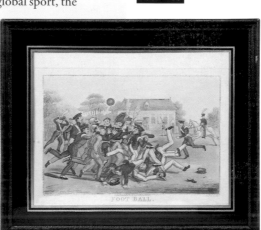

▼ This picture by Robert Crookshank is believed to be the earliest known image of football in Britain, and this example was engraved by Geoffrey Hunt, and published in 1827. It shows an unsophisticated soldiers' friendly match more reminiscent of a battle. The authorities tried to ban this type of "mob football", but the game continued, and gradually rules and regulations were applied.

£300-400

▲ Painted with alternate maroon and white panels, this leather football is inscribed "This ball was used in the Scottish Cup final, Third Lanark 3 Rangers 1, 1904-5, at New Hampden". Commemorative footballs such as this, decorated in the team colours and inscribed with match details, are often found in the trophy cabinets of football clubs and players. Third Lanark were members of the Scottish League for 77 years until the team went into liquidation in 1967.

£600-800

▼ Made in around 1900, this Continental briar pipe measuring 4¾ in (12cm) from tip to toe, carved in the shape of an eight-panel football resting on a stem made to resemble a football boot, was probably manufactured in Germany. Pipes with carved bowls, initially made from meerschaum (a fine, light clay) from Germany, were first popularized in Britain in the 1830s.

£80-120

◄ Made from crepe paper, this unofficial programme and souvenir is unusual in football, but the design, which celebrates the 1906 FA Cup final is characteristic of the period. In this match, Everton achieved their first FA Cup success, beating Newcastle United 1-0.

£150-200

◄ Dated 5 March 1909, this very unusual piece is a City of Manchester tenancy agreement, entered into by Manchester United for the land on which Old Trafford was to be built. Architect Archibald Leitch designed the stadium which was opened in 1910.

£150-200

▼ Many games have been produced that attempt to simulate football. This 1920s game, "Finga-Foota", was manufactured by Broda Jenkins & Co at Brentford, Middlesex, and features cardboard cut-outs of six well-known personalities of the day, including "Old Bill", Bruce Bairnsfather's comical World War 1 character, Lloyd George, Charlie Chaplin and Admiral Jellico. The game also comprised two goals, three pairs each of red and white football boots, to be worn on the finger, and a green baize table-top football pitch.

£100-150

▼ Bearing the inscription "Guid Auld Killie", this moulded glass pint tankard was made to commemorate Kilmarnock winning the Scottish Cup on 17 April 1920.

£60-80

▲ FA official H.A. Ayling amassed a collection of 22 FA steward's lapel badges during his time as a referee between 1897 and 1932. The items shown here include three FA steward's ribboned and gilt-tasslled lapel badges, 1910-13; a red, white and blue silk FA committee member's rosette; and four gilt-metal and enamel Football Association steward's lapel badges, 1929-32.

£400-600

Miscellaneous Ephemera 2

Collectors of all sorts of different subjects – football, cricket, motoring, shipping, toys, literature, and so on – soon discover that the more they collect, the more there is to collect, and that one interest soon leads to another. For example, a fan living in Devon who has a general interest in football and collects the programmes of Exeter City, Plymouth Argyle, Torquay United and Tiverton Town, might also collect the colourful commemorative football rugs that were produced a few miles away, in Axminster, or the rare souvenir and commemorative football china produced by the local potteries at Torquay, Barnstaple and Dartmouth. Similarly, collectors who specialize in football shirts and jerseys may also collect the embroidered badges and motifs that used to adorn the shirts and jerseys, and this in turn might lead them to collect the enam-

elled metal pin badges issued to clubs and officials. Many fabulous collections of football memorabilia, however, know no bounds, and display a wide diversity of objects that reveal the interests of the collector.

▲ These football badges once belonged to the great Alex James who represented Scotland between 1926 and 1933: (top left) Scotland v England, 1928-29; (top right) Scotland v Wales, 1929-30; (bottom right) Wales international; (centre) Ireland international; (bottom left) Arsenal 1930 FA Cup final.

£150-200

◀ The famous Everton player William "Dixie" Dean was presented with this illuminated address, dated 22 January 1928, by the people of Birkenhead on his 21st birthday. Even at this young age, Dean was already a great name in English football; he scored 12 goals in his first five games for England. He scored a record 379 League goals during a career that began with Tranmere Rovers in 1923-24, and ended with Notts County in 1938-39.

£400-600

▲ A formal presentation piece, this illuminated address was given to Arsenal's Jack Lambert following the 1930 FA Cup final by the inhabitants of his home town. In 1929-30 Arsenal won the FA Cup for the first time.

£200-300

► Ariel Productions Limited produced this football board-game, "The Game of Wembley", inspired by the FA Cup, during the 1950s and 1960s. Played in a similar way to the ever-popular "Monopoly" (produced by Waddington), the game included Wembley money, draw cards and team-strip cards. This game is not rare and examples can still be discovered in bric-a-brac shops today, although collectors would be very lucky to find a complete game in such good condition as the one illustrated here.

£30-50

◄ This high quality Axminster Victory rug was produced to commemorate the achievements of Celtic FC during season 1966-67 when they won five trophies. Nowadays souvenir rugs similar to this are quite commonly available from supporters' shops and other football club merchandise retailers.

£120-180

▼ Drawn by Henry Mayo Bateman, this cartoon is called "The Football Match, The Man Who Stopped To Smoke A Bar One." Cartoons in this style were popular during the 1950s and 1960s.

£500-1,000

▲ First produced during the 1980s, phonecards have become collectable items in the way that cigarette cards were popular during the first half of the century. These recent cards from England, Italy, Japan and America show the type of football phone cards that are likely to increase in value.

£5-50 each

Works of Art

The title of "Works of Art" in the context of soccer is a bit of a misnomer when used to describe decorative objects produced to celebrate our national game. Whilst other popular British sports including Cricket, Golf, Tennis, Fishing and Boxing have inspired painters, potters and metalsmiths to produce many works of true artistic merit, the game of football has by and large failed to do so. Cricket has been commonly represented by potters with ceramic figures and other china such as plates and vases; golf inspired many sculptors; tennis was represented in jewellery; and fishing and boxing often feature in paintings and prints. Football art on the other hand seems to have been generally overlooked. The reason for this remains a mystery, although many football historians and collectors believe this apparent artistic oversight is closely related to the bad publicity that football received during World War 1, which also lead many English public schools to drop the game in favour of Rugby football.

Despite the outbreak of war with Germany in 1914, the Football Association permitted the 1914-15 season FA Cup competition to run its course, culminating in the gloomy "Khaki Cup final" between Sheffield United and Chelsea, and the Football League programme was not halted either, resulting in charges of unpatriotism from the press and other quarters. In fact, by early 1915, the FA had encouraged 500,000 men to join the forces – a contribution not matched by any other section of the community. But after end of hostilities the belief persisted that rugby players had been more patriotic in 1914. This was followed by a swing away from football together with a decline in the number of those gentlemen footballers who had played such an important role in the creation of the modern game. Thus football lost the support of the social class that was likely to have commissioned or demanded football works of art, and so football became increasingly a working class game.

Another reason that football does not feature in many works of art is that it has always been a male-dominated game, and historically was not widely watched or played by women in the same way that golf was for example, although women's football clubs have been in existence since the 1890s. However, female participation in the game has been restrained more by the physical demands of the game than by officialdom, though their contribution was not officially recognised by the Football Association until 1969. Therefore football, unlike cricket, golf or tennis, has not been widely represented by the art of jewellers or the crafters of precious metals.

Collectors of football memorabilia soon discover that any real football works of art deserving of this description, tend to date from before World War 1, and are usually very rare and very expensive. Most "artistic" pieces though, are of a much later date and are more notable for being uncommon than for their quality. Pictures are usually prints, football-related china usually comprises mass-market, transfer-printed plates, mugs and other tablewares manufactured between the 1930, and the present day, and metalware often takes the form of spelter figures reproducing rare, high quality bronze originals. Football jewellery is almost non-existent, while the products of silversmiths and goldsmiths rarely appear except as football trophies and medals (see Caps & Awards pp.110-117). Sadly, these trends still apply today. Occasionally interesting pieces do appear however, such as Victorian umbrella stands, highly collectable lead figures of football teams, and dinner services made for use by the Football Association featuring their shield.

Left: A Dartmouth Pottery brown-glazed tankard decorated with a footballer. *Background image:* A late 19th century clay tobacco-smoking pipe. The bowl is moulded with football players of the period wearing breeches and the hand support is modelled as a football and boot. *Above:* A 1930s French bronze figure of a footballer signed J.A. Reg.

Chinaware

It is fortunate that Great Britain has a tradition of producing commemorative china stretching back many hundreds of years, and that regardless of what people collect – be it for example royal memorabilia, sporting memorabilia or railway memorabilia, we can be sure that a potter or porcelain company somewhere has produced a ceramic commemorative to celebrate some aspect of it. Football is no exception. Collectors of football memorabilia can choose from a reasonable range of football-related china produced to commemorate the game from its earliest years to the present day. Through a small host of mugs, plates, plaques and figures the history of Association Football can be followed: from 19th century mugs decorated with simple, transfer-printed portraits, through to the clever character-jugs of today, featuring the football heroes of the late 20th century. Whilst most pieces can be obtained for less than £200, with only the exceptionally rare or beautiful pieces commanding higher prices, it is important for collectors to be aware of the existence of damaged or restored pieces and reproductions, and be careful when buying.

▲ These three pieces are representative of the many hundreds of small decorative china models, made as inexpensive gifts and souvenirs, that first became popular during the 1880s. From left to right: a Carlton Ware model of the FA Cup painted with the arms of Bournemouth; a football with the arms of Ewell; and an FA Cup by Arcadian China with the arms of Reading.

£15-20 each

◄ The origin of the early football scene depicted on this 19th century Staffordshire mug has been disputed by collectors and football historians. Some believe the picture represents an early England-Scotland international match; the first of these was played in the spring of 1873. It could also depict one of the first FA Cup Finals. Another theory is that it may depict the Old Etonians FC, the last amateur side to achieve a good degree of success.

£100-150

► It was the football teams from the industrial north that dominated English football during the late 19th and early 20th centuries, and the popularity of the game inspired the pottery factories

scattered around Stoke-on-Trent to produce many types of mug similar to this, featuring portraits of ten north-country players.

£100-150

▼ This attractive transfer printed plate, designed by F.J. Kepple for the Bristol Porcelain & Glass Company, was made to commemorate the 1906-07 season, and is quite rare and very collectable. The gilt line decoration around the moulded rim is a sign of the high quality of the piece. In this year Newcastle United won the League Championship, and The Wednesday achieved a 2-1 victory over Everton in the FA Cup final.

£200-300

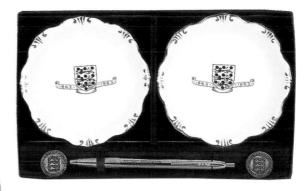

▲ The FA produced many souvenirs to celebrate their Centenary in 1963. Presentation sets of items however, such as this one comprising two ash trays, two badges and an inscribed pen, were only available to employees and officials of the FA.

£50-80

► Terry Curran and the other members of Everton FC were presented with this Minton blue and gilt-embellished porcelain bowl to commemorate their achievements in 1983-84. During this season they won the FA Cup, beating Watford 2-0, and were runners-up in the Milk Cup, losing 1-0 to Liverpool in the replay.

£250-300

▲ Art Deco novelty teapots such as this one by Sadler's of Burslem, were popular for many years: the body has been made in the shape of a football, the handle is a player taking a throw-in, the spout is a referee's whistle, and the finial represents the FA Cup. This example has been made in the colours of Plymouth Argyle FC.

£100-150

◄ The shield of the English Football Association appears on dinner ware used for their official occasions and on presentation items. These pieces of Royal Worcester "Viceroy" bone china, for example, were probably used at a banquet given by the FA prior to the 1966 World Cup finals held in England.

£200-300

Metalware

For many centuries artists, sculptors and smiths have been forming decorative objects and works of art from metals such as gold, silver, bronze, brass and iron. More recently, and particularly since the Industrial Revolution during the 19th century, new metals and alloys including spelter and aluminium have been developed, which have also been used to manufacture decorative objects and figures. The growth of football in this country has coincided with the development of these new metals and the mass-production of everyday metal objects and decoration. Sculptors, metal-smiths and foundries turned to football for inspiration to decorate a wide range of objects. More collectable items are made from precious metals and bronzes. Be wary when collecting some types of metalware, particularly bronze, spelter and cast-iron objects and figures. Spelter is often patinated to resemble bronze and can be mistaken for the real thing. Spelter figures are also easy to copy and are being reproduced in the Far East, made from light-weight, painted alloy.

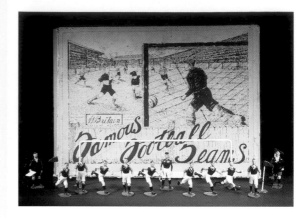

▲ William Britain's toy company is one of the oldest in the United Kingdom, and Britain's hollow-cast metal model soldiers and other metal toys still enjoy worldwide fame. In the 1920s Britains produced an excellent series of "Famous Football Teams" including England, Scotland and Holland, painted in the team colours. Set 187 featured Aston Villa.

£200-300

◄ A late Victorian piece, the back of this painted cast-iron umbrella and walking-stick stand features a central figure of a footballer holding a ball, and inscribed above with the word "Footballer". During the second half of the 19th century, cast-iron was used to make a wide variety of different objects.

£400-600

► This lithographed metal biscuit tin is decorated in colours to celebrate the FA Cup and commemorate the 1926-27 final between Arsenal and Cardiff. The tin is inscribed with English and Scottish League honours since 1900, the story of FA Cup winners and features three footballing scenes.

£40-60

◄ Many people today are surprised to learn that images of football found its way onto jewellery and works of art of the late 19th and early 20th century. During this early period however, football was regarded as a fashionable pastime, and this encouraged people to commission decorative pieces featuring football motifs. This vesta-case, a practical fashion accessory of its day designed to hold matches, was made to hang from the chain of a pocket watch.

£200-300

▼ Made in South America in the 1930s, this piece is a brass fob-watch stand modelled as a figure of a football player; the watch was suspended from the hook at the end of the figure's left arm. This figure is believed to represent the Argentinian forward, Carlos Peucelle, who scored in the first World Cup final in 1930, although Argentina lost.

£100-150

► Made by W. Kershaw in 1971, this bronze sculpture was commissioned to commemorate Manchester United winning the European Cup in 1968. The piece originally cost £175 and represents Bobby Charlton, George Best and Denis Law.

£500-800

▲ This 1930s spelter figure of a footballer taking a throw-in, was probably once part of a three-piece spelter clock garniture, comprising two spelter figures of footballers designed to flank a spelter clock that was also decorated with a figure of a football player. Unfortunately, over the years, many garnitures were dismantled, and collectors today often discover only single figures. When collecting spelter, be aware that pieces can suffer from "spelter disease", a form of surface oxidization which may produce bubbles.

£120-180

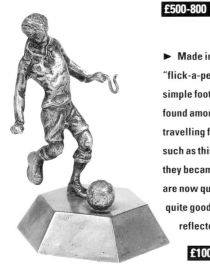

► Made in the 1950s, this painted, metal-alloy "flick-a-penny" football figure is typical of many simple football-inspired games once commonly found amongst the smaller attractions at travelling fairgrounds. Over the years items such as this were often thrown away because they became damaged or unfashionable and so are now quite rare. This example is in quite good condition, and this fact is reflected in the price.

£100-150

Caps & Awards

Footballers everywhere, whether schoolboy, amateur or professional, play the game to win. The object of their endeavour is invariably to help their team win a League or Division Championship, or succeed in a Cup competition of some description. Apart from the immense satisfaction of beating other teams, the focus of many football competitions is some sort of trophy – the physical expression of their victory. Most trophies take the form of a cup, either of silver or gold, which is loaned to the victorious club for about a year to show off in their trophy cabinet. The players on the other hand are each awarded small commemorative medals or miniature copies of the trophy which they usually keep and cherish throughout their lives. These trophies and medals represent the highlights in a club's history and of a footballer's career and are very sought after by collectors of football memorabilia.

Within British professional football the most important domestic competitions in both England and

Scotland are the four national League Championships and the Football Association Challenge Cups, which date back to the earliest days of organized football during the last century. On the European stage it is the European Champion Clubs Cup (to give the European Cup competition its full title) that enjoys the most prestige, while internationally the FIFA World Cup continues to be the football tournament that every nation and player wants to compete in and win. Though these latter competitions, and others similar to them, are not old in an historic football sense, European and international competition medals and trophies are much rarer than examples from domestic football and are highly valued and much sought after by collectors all over the world.

Collectors also count representative caps and jerseys as "awards" on the basis that selection for an international or representative game is an honour bestowed upon deserving players in recognition of their footballing qualities. Caps are awarded to a player for each appearance in a national side and are symbolic of the game or games he has played. They are usually made up of a velveteen type material, typically inscribed and decorated in gold or silver braid with season/date, badge, and tassel. Contrary to popular belief these caps were never actually designed to be worn as head-gear, being of a universal small size and only ever "worn" for official portrait purposes. Caps were awarded for many representative and international games including Full Internationals, Under-21, FA Schools and Youth Internationals, Trials and Amateurs. They are all collectable, and their values depend upon the game's status and the identity and fame of the players concerned.

Shirts or jerseys awarded to players are also very popular amongst collectors, and have the additional interest of having been worn by a player during a game of representative or international standard. Some are even offered for sale in their post-match unwashed state and are left in this condition by the purest collectors! In addition, players often swap their jerseys with their opposite number after memorable games as a memento of the encounter. These swapped shirts are as keenly sought after by collectors as they are prized by players. For example, Bobby Moore, captain of West Ham United and England during periods of the 1960s and 1970s and capped on 108 occasions, was once asked what his most prized possession was. He had no hesitation in declaring that it was the jersey he swapped with Pele following the memorable England v Brazil game in the 1970 World Cup finals in Mexico.

Left: **A London Cup winner's medal awarded to Jim Standen of Arsenal during the 1957-58 season.** *Background image:* **An FA international gold medal medal engraved "F.W. Kean 1922-23" with fitted case.** *Above:* **A blue England v Wales international cap awarded during the 1954-55 Home International Championship.**

Medals 1

The pinnacle of many a footballer's career is being part of a team winning a major competition. The winners of the Football League (now the Premier League) or the FA Cup nowadays qualify for prestigious European competitions such as the European Cup, the Cup Winners Cup and the UEFA Cup. Football clubs successful in any of these competitions, are awarded trophies or shields which they normally keep for 12 months to display in the boardroom's trophy cabinet. At the same time, the winning players traditionally receive medals. In the most important competitions medals are presented to players of the beaten finalists or runners-up team as well. Unfortunately collectors do not often get the chance to obtain football medals presented at major competitions or awarded to star players. However, on the rare occasions that famous players' medals are offered for sale, they often realize a lot of money – certainly a great deal more than their gold or silver content would otherwise justify.

► This 15ct gold medal was gained by Tommy Crawshaw of The Wednesday following the Scotland-England Inter-League match in 1895, that was won by The English League 4-1. The first official Inter-League game to be played took place on 11 April 1892, and the last match took place at Hampden Park on 17 March 1976, when the Football League won 1-0 in front of only 9,000 spectators.

£150-200

◄ Inscribed and dated 1888-89, this silver Scottish Football Association Challenge Cup runners-up · medal was awarded to Celtic player Tom Maley following a Cup final replay between Celtic and Third Lanark. The previous game had been played in a snow-storm, and although Third Lanark won this match 3-0 it was declared void. Maley had spells with Hibernian, Partick Thistle and Third Lanark, before joining Celtic in 1888. He later went on to manage Manchester City and Bradford. He died in 1935.

£800-1,200

▼ Goalkeeper John Dickson received this silver winner's medal when Queen's Park FC became the first winners of the Scottish FA Cup in 1874, following a controversial match in which a Clydesdale goal was disallowed. In those days there were no nets and the crowd lined the pitch. On this occasion Queen's Park's opponents Clydesdale "scored" after the ball rebounded off a spectator and back into play. The referee subsequently disallowed the goal.

£800-1,200

▶ Manchester United won their first-ever Division 1 Championship in season 1907-08, just two seasons after being promoted from Division 2, and this 15ct gold Football League Championship winner's medal was awarded to goalkeeper Harry Moger. Moger joined Manchester United in 1903, and appeared in 242 League and 22 Cup matches, until he retired from football in 1912.

£1,200-1,800

▼ From the 1895-96 season, this FA Cup winner's medal, presented to Tommy Crawshaw of The Wednesday, is inscribed, "Winners of the Eng. Assoc. Cup, 1895-6, T.H. Crawshaw". The 1896 final marked the first 25 years of the competition, and the first presentation of the replacement Challenge Cup trophy: the original FA Cup was stolen in 1895. The Wednesday won their first FA Cup Final in this year beating Wolverhampton Wanderers 2-1.

£1,500-2,000

▲ Sheffield Wednesday (then just The Wednesday) won their first League Championship with 42 points in the 1902-03 season, finishing ahead of Aston Villa (41 points), and this 15ct gold winner's medal was presented to Tommy Crawshaw. The Wednesday also won the Championship the following season ahead of Manchester City. The style of League Championship winner's medals has changed frequently throughout the history of the competition.

£800-1,200

▼ An unofficial piece, this medal was awarded to the players of Bury FC who achieved an incredible 6-0 victory over Derby County in the 1902-03 FA Cup final at Crystal Palace.

£400-600

▲ The 1908 Charity Shield match, the first in its current form, was played at Stamford Bridge between Manchester United (League Champions) and Queen's Park Rangers (Southern League Champions). United won 4-1 in a replay, after a 1-1 draw.

£600-800

Medals 2

No-one can be sure when the first medals were awarded in the game of Association Football, however it is clear that medals were awarded at most major competitions from the outset and that traditionally they have been of gold or silver-gilt. Prior to the World War 1, players often had the choice of a medal or a pocket watch or even money! Surprisingly, players who chose medals sometimes had to have them engraved themselves and at their own expense! It is sad therefore to appreciate that over the years huge numbers of football medals of all types, shapes and sizes and awarded to players at all levels of football competitions, have either been lost or sold to jewellers for scrap value. To many collectors of football memorabilia, the career of the medal winner is every bit as important as the medal itself, while the fame and world standing of the recipient often affects the value of a medal or collection of medals. Some players have won large collections of medals. Three 19th century players won five FA Cup winner's medals each: Charles Wollaston, Lord Kinnaird and James Forrest.

▶ Arsenal beat Huddersfield Town 2-0 to win the FA Cup on 26 April 1930, and this 15ct gold medal was presented to Alex James. It was Arsenal's first major homour, and James scored the first goal in the final. Born in Lanarkshire in 1901, James joined Arsenal from Preston North End in 1929, and was capped eight times for Scotland.

£1,000-1,500

◀ After Linfield FC finished the 1934-35 season top of the Irish League, this medal was awarded to John "Soldier" Jones, Linfield's much-capped Northern Ireland international. The Irish League was set up in 1890, and featured Clarence, Cliftonville, Distillery, Glentoran, Linfield, Milford, Old Park and Ulster as founder members. Linfield were the first League Champions in 1891, and since then have dominated the Irish League by winning the competition over 40 times.

£250-350

▼ Third Lanark Athletic FC was one of the original eight clubs who formed the Scottish Football Association in 1873, and also one of the 14 clubs invited to start the Scottish League in 1890. Due to financial problems the team dropped out of the League at the end of 1966-67, leaving Queen's Park as the sole survivor of the original eight sides. This gold and enamel League Division 2 Championship medal was awarded to J. McFarlane after the 1930-31 season.

£250-300

▲ This 9ct gold 1953 FA Cup winner's medal is inscribed on the reverse "The Football Association, Challenge Cup, Winners, Stanley Mortensen". In this game Blackpool staged a remarkable comeback from 3-1 down, to beat Bolton Wanderers 4-3, after a unique Wembley hat-trick by Stan Mortensen.

£9,000-10,000

▼ Although Manchester United's Dennis Viollet did not play in the 1956-57 FA Cup final because of an injury, he was presented with a special medal by Manchester United Football Club to commemorate his significant participation in helping the "Red Devils" reach the final. On the day the team was beaten 2-1 by Aston Villa, largely because after six minutes United's goalkeeper, Ray Wood, was carried off after breaking a cheek bone in a collision with Ason Villa's Peter McParland. Unofficial commemorative medals such as this are unusual, and so are of particular interest to collectors.

£300-500

▲ The European Cup Winners Cup competition, first contested in 1960-61, usually includes from the British Isles and Eire the winners of the FA Cup, Scottish FA Cup, Welsh FA Cup, Irish FA Cup and FA of Ireland Cup. The 1964-65 Cup Winners Cup final was played between West Ham United and TSV Munich on 19 May 1965. This 18ct gold and enamel medal is one of those awarded to West Ham players after winning the match 2-0. Both goals were scored by Alan Sealey.

£4,000-6,000

▼ Less expensive to collect than medals from major competitions, local medals such as this Glasgow Cup winner's medal presented to Archie Macauley of Rangers in 1937, are often made to a high standard.

£200-300

Medals 3

Collectors of soccer memorabilia who specialize in soccer medals soon discover many interesting facts and feats concerning these awards: who won what, where, when and how many? It is these details that bring medals to life. For example, Jimmy Delaney, Scotland's international outside-right (1936-48), created a unique record by gaining Scotland, England, Northern Ireland and Eire FA Cup final medals over a period of 19 years. Today, FA Cup medals are made from 9ct gold. However when the FA Cup competition was resumed after World War 2, the members of Charlton Athletic's team, which was defeated 4-1 by Derby County in the 1946 Cup final, each received two medals! Gold was scarce at the time, and so the Charlton Athletic team was presented with bronze runners-up medals; the gold medals came later. The European Cup is one of the world's most prestigious football competitions, and the memorabilia and medals connected with the tournament are amongst the most popular and expensive to collect.

◀ On 25 May 1967, Celtic FC became the first British club and the only Scottish club so far, to win the coveted European Cup. Team members received this 18ct gold, and red and blue enamel medal after beating Inter-Milan 2-1.

£8,000-12,000

◀ Celtic completed a remarkable grand slam in the 1966-67 season, by winning the Scottish Football League (for the 22nd time with 58 points), the Scottish FA Cup (beating Aberdeen 2-0), the Scottish League Cup (beating Rangers 1-0), and the Glasgow Cup. The team then became the first British club to win the European Cup. This Scottish Football League Championship Division 1 gold and enamel medal (above left), was awarded to Tommy Gemmell, the full-back who was famous for his long-range shooting. It was this ability that enabled him to score one of Celtic's two goals in the European Cup victory over Inter-Milan in the 1967 final (see above).

£500-700

▼ First contested in the 1873-74 season , this winner's medal from the Scottish FA Cup competition 1968-69, was awarded to the players of Celtic following a 4-0 win over Rangers on 26 April 1969. Since the 1890s the Scottish Cup has been dominated by Celtic and Rangers. Up to and including the 1993-94 season, Celtic has won 29 times (runners-up 16 times), and Rangers on 26 occasions (runners-up 16 times).

£600-800

▼ In 1958-59 fourth Divison was created from the bottom halves of the two third Divisions (North and South). This winner's medal from the new Division 3 (comprising the top halves of the two old divisions), was awarded to a Sunderland player in 1987-88.

£250-350

▲ In 1974 the FA introduced the Challenge Vase to replace the FA Amateur Challenge Cup (1894-1974). This competition is open to non-Football League clubs, but excludes those competing in the FA Challenge Trophy. Hoddesdon Town were the first winners in 1975. Medals awarded for non-League competitions are usually cast in silver, such as this runners-up medal from 1974-75 awarded to Epsom & Ewell, rather than gold, and are less expensive to collect than medals awarded for better-known competitions.

£150-200

▼ On 5 May 1983, the Japanese company Canon UK Ltd took over the sponsorship of the Football League for a three-year period. At the time, it was Britain's richest sporting sponsorship. Amongst the prize money available to clubs was £50,000 to the Division 1 Champions, £25,000 to the runners-up, and £15,000 to the team in third place. Everton won the Division 1 Championship the following season, 1984-85, with 90 points, ahead of their Merseyside rivals Liverpool, with 77 points. This 9ct gold and enamel winner's medal, inscribed "Canon League Division 1, Winners" was awarded to Torry Curran.

£800-1,000

▲ The 1973-74 Scottish League Cup was won by Dundee, and this is one of the official winner's medals. This tournament began during World War 2 (called the Scottish Southern League Cup), but was officially founded in 1946-47.

£400-600

Trophies

It would not be fair to pretend here that any of the major football competition trophies have ever turned up for sale or are ever likely to! However, many minor League or decorative trophies and shields from long-defunct competitions do come on to the market from time-to-time, together with replica trophies presented to players of successful teams. Many trophies have interesting histories – for example, the "Little Tin Idol" – the original FA Cup trophy, which was made in 1872 by Messrs Martin Hall & Co and cost about £20, was stolen from the window of a firm of football outfitters in Birmingham in 1895. It was never recovered, but in 1958 an 83 year-old man claimed that he had stolen the cup in order to melt it down to make counterfeit half-crowns! Similarly, the Jules Rimet World Cup trophy was stolen from a cabinet in Central Hall, Westminster, on 20 March 1966, during a stamp exhibition prior to the World Cup tournament in England. The FA received a ransom demand for the trophy, while the police made great efforts to locate it. Eventually, a black and white mongrel called Pickles found the trophy under a bush on Beulah Hill in south London. Both dog and owner received rewards – including a medal, a film role and a year's supply of treats for Pickles.

▶ A good quality amateur trophy, this silver and oak shield made for the Glasgow and District Churches Football League (Reserve Section), has been embossed with a central footballing scene enclosed by circular silver plaques.

£150-250

▶ William Ralph "Dixie" Dean (Everton and England) received this shield from the Everton FC Supporters Club to commemorate his League goal-scoring record of 60 goals during the 1927-28 season. The 29 circular discs surrounding the central engraved plaque, represent the matches played during that season, and Dean has marked his favourite game (a 3-3 draw against Liverpool on 25 February 1928, in which he scored a hat-trick) with a white arrow.

£500-700

▲ Presented to Alfred John Bishop, a member of FA Cup winning team Wolves in 1908, this silver replica of the "Little Tin Idol", the first FA Cup, is one of eleven that were produced.

£400-600

► Dennis Viollet of Manchester United was awarded this bakelite and silver FA Charity Shield plaque following a match against Manchester City on 24 October 1956. Charity Shield games, traditionally played between the League Champions and the FA Cup winners, are now played at the start of the new season, with proceeds going to charity.

£400-600

▲ Made from Britannia metal, this late 19th century Australian football trophy was presented to Cassilis, winners of the Omro District and Football Association 1898. Britannia metal is an alloy of tin, antimony and copper, and was used in the 19th century as a substitute for pewter. A low-profile side, the Australians did qualify for the 1974 World Cup, and went close in 1994. Craig Johnson (Liverpool) and Tony Dorigo (Chelsea and Leeds) are Australians who have recently played in the League.

£100-150

► This silver-plated trophy was presented to George Cummings of Partick Thistle (later Aston Villa) by the Scottish FA to commemorate Scotland's victory in the Home International Championship during the 1935-36 season. Cummings made nine appearances for Scotland 1935-39, and gained one wartime international cap.

£80-120

▲ Made by Abel Lafleur, the sculptor of the original World Cup, the Jules Rimet trophy, this bronze rectangular plaque commemorates a match between France and Wales on 25 May 1933. The game, Wales' first international against an overseas side, ended in a 1-1 draw. Smaller versions than this 16in (40.6cm) piece were also made for each player.

£500-700

▼ Stan Mortensen was presented with this silver miniature replica of the FA Cup by Blackpool FC after their victory in 1953. The 1953 Cup final is often referred to as the "Matthews Final", because the great English footballer Stanley Matthews finally carried off his first winner's medal.

£200-300

Caps 1

International and representative caps, awarded to players for appearances in their national side, are amongst the most highly valued and collectable items of football memorabilia. Like medals and jerseys, football caps have the special attraction and interest of having been won or worn by actual players. The first "official" international football match took place in Glasgow on 30 November 1872, and was billed as Scotland against England. The result was a goalless draw. The first England international caps, which were royal blue in colour and decorated with the rose emblem, were awarded in 1886 at the suggestion of N. Lane Jackson, the assistant secretary of the Football Association and founder of Corinthians – the celebrated English amateur football team. The caps were later embellished with gold braid and a tassel and other colours were used; eventually the rose emblem was replaced with the familiar three lions badge.

▲ These four International caps were awarded to Steve Bloomer (Derby Country and Middlesborough) between 1895 and 1905. He is widely credited as being the first outstanding goal-scorer. His 28 goals for England from 23 international matches between 1895 and 1907, remained a record until 1958. In addition he scored 297 League goals for Derby County (1892-1906 and 1910-14), and 55 for Middlesborough (1906-10), from a total of 600 appearances before retiring in 1914.

£300-500 each

▼ Billy Meredith was awarded this green Welsh international cap for his three international appearances in 1903 against England, Scotland and Ireland. His career spanned 30 years (1894-1924), during which he played for Manchester City and Manchester United, and scored 181 League and 56 Cup goals. He represented Wales on 48 occasions, scoring 11 goals.

£400-600

► Harry Makepeace of Everton FC was the recipient of this purple England v Scotland International cap, for the match at Hampden Park, Glasgow on 23 March 1912. The teams drew 1-1. Harry Makepeace played for the English national side four times between 1906 and 1912. He was also capped for England at cricket, and made a Test century in Australia.

£150-200

▲ Also awarded to Harry Makepeace (see above), this cap was made for the 1911-12 Home International Championship match between England and Wales, played on 11 March 1912 at Wrexham, England won 2-0.. Wales were unable to win any of their Home International fixtures and finished bottom of the table, while Scotland and England shared the trophy in this year.

£150-200

▼ This England v Belgium international cap 1923, was awarded to Fred Kean of The Wednesday (see above right). England won this match 6-1, at Highbury on 19 March. Although Kean had lost his place as half-back in The Wednesday team at this time, he was still picked England. Kean began his career with Sheffield Hallam, playing for Portsmouth after World War 1, before signing for Wednesday and returning to Sheffield.

£200-300

▼ In 1929, England played a three match, end-of-season tour of Europe, beating France and Belgium 5-1, but losing to Spain, their first ever defeat by a foreign country. This cap was awarded to Fred Kean of Bolton Wanderers for this game. Kean played in two of the three tour matches, and made nine appearances for England 1923-29, while playing for The Wednesday and Bolton Wanderers.

£300-400

▲ Jack Crayston of Arsenal received this maroon, yellow and black England v Germany cap for a match held on 4 December 1935; England defeated Germany 3-0. In the 1930s Crayston made eight international appearances for England and played for the Football League. Crayston joined Arsenal from Barrow in May 1934. During his time with Arsenal he won two Championship medals (1934-35, 1937-38), and an FA Cup winner's medal (1936).

£200-300

► The Irish Football Association was formed in November 1880, through the determination of J. M. McAlery, a keen Belfast sportsman. Ireland played their first match against England on 18 February 1882, and the team lost 13-0. This Northern Ireland international cap was awarded during the 1936-37 Home International Championship, when Northern Ireland lost all their three matches: 1-3 to England, 1-3 to Scotland and 1-4 to Wales.

£200-300

Caps 2

Most full international caps have a value of between £200 and £500 each, depending on the player to whom the cap was awarded, and the occasion or match that it represents. These two criteria are very important to collectors because caps as objects have little intrinsic value. Therefore, a cap awarded to a celebrated international player who, perhaps, holds the record for international goals or appearances for his country, will generally be far more valuable and desirable than, say, one awarded to a player whose one and only appearance was as a substitute during a "friendly" international. In 1959 Billy Wright (Wolverhampton Wanderers) became the first British player to win 100 caps. Kenny Dalglish (Celtic and Liverpool) became the first Scot to collect 100 caps, while Pat Jennings (Watford, Tottenham Hotspur and Arsenal) achieved the feat for Northern Ireland in 1983. Peter Shilton curren-tly holds the record for England caps. It is also possible to make interesting "theme" collections of caps relating to unusual occurrences, such as England players who have been sent off during internationals, players capped for England whilst on the books of a foreign club – once quite a rarity but now quite common, and players from the lower divisions chosen to represent their country in full internationals.

▼ Between 26 October and 16 November 1938, England successfully contested three International matches, scoring 14 goals and conceding none. This cap is from a game against Norway on 9 November, that England won 4-0. The other two matches were played against a FIFA team, and Northern Ireland. More recently, Norway did much to prevent England qualifying for the 1994 World Cup Finals.

£200-300

▲ England's first international after World War II was played on 28 September 1946 against Northern Ireland in Belfast, and this cap was awarded for that game. Of those who had played in the last pre-war international, against Romania in Bucharest on 24 May 1939, only Tommy Lawton remained. England won 7-2 in Belfast that day, and for Billy Wright the match marked the beginning of an international career that was to last 13 years.

£200-300

► England first played Wales on Saturday 18 January 1879 at The Oval, and defeated the visitors 2-1. Since then the two sides have met many times, usually during the now-defunct Home International Championship. This England-Wales cap is from the 1952-53 Home Championship match played on 12 November 1952, that resulted in a 5-2 victory for England. Wales won the Home International Championship seven times.

£200-300

◄ Dennis Viollet received this England v Luxembourg cap for his appearance for in a 1961 World Cup qualifying game at Highbury. Following a 4-1 victory in this game (the team had already won the first leg 9-0), England went on to be the only British representatives at the 1962 World Cup in Chile, and progressed as far as the quarter-finals before being knocked out by Brazil, who went on to win the trophy.

£300-400

▲ This blue Scottish International cap was presented for the 1952-53 Home International Championship. In this year the trophy was shared between Scotland and England. When the last tournament was contested in 1984, the Championship had been played for 88 times – England having won 34 times, Scotland 24, Wales 7 and Northern Ireland 3. There were 20 shared titles.

£150-200

▼ Awarded to Frank Gray, this blue Scotland international cap, 1980-81, represents his six international appearances in 1981, including three World Cup qualifying matches. Between 1976 and 1983 Frank Gray wore the dark blue Scotland jersey on 32 occasions and participated in the ill-fated 1982 World Cup finals in Spain, when Scotland failed to qualify for the latter stages on goal difference.

£300-400

▲ Roy Vernon received this red Wales international cap, 1964-65 shortly after he had joined Stoke City from Everton, and represents his three international appearances in 1965 against Northern Ireland (Home International Championship), Greece (World Cup qualifying match) and Italy (friendly). Vernon made 32 appearances for Wales between 1957 and 1968

£300-400

► Another Welsh cap (see above), this Under-23 example was awarded for the 1982-83 season. More recent caps such as this one, are difficult to find as it may be many years before they are released into the collectors market. Caps like this one show the variation in styles and designs in the different categories of British football, and can form an interesting collection.

£140-160

▲ Matches known as intermediate internationals are played by, for example, the England Under-23 team or the England "B" team, and this cap was awarded for a game played at Highbury on 2 January 1973 against the Netherlands. The result was a 3-1 win for England: Dennis Mortimer (Coventry City) scored twice for England, while Trevor Whymark (Ipswich Town) scored the other.

£200-300

Jerseys 1

Since football in all its various forms became organized during the mid-1800s, football shirts or jerseys have been worn by footballers to identify themselves from players of other teams. Indeed, in many instances the colour or style of jerseys chosen by teams to play in have resulted in their nicknames today, such as Coventry "Sky Blues", Norwich City "Canaries", and Tottenham Hotspur "Lily-whites". Herbert Chapman, Arsenal's manager between 1925 and 1934, tried out numbered shirts for the first time on 25 August 1928 at Hillsborough. Chapman's experiment was followed by the first numbering of shirts in the 1933 FA Cup final on 29 April, when Everton wore numbers 1-11 and Manchester City 12-22. The English and Scottish Leagues began to use numbered shirts at the start of the 1939-40 season. Celtic, however, have always refused to number their players' shirts in domestic matches, although UEFA insist that they number shirts for European competitions.

▶ A good example of a shirt from the mid-1930s, this red and white Arsenal FC jersey was probably worn Alex James. Arsenal dominated English football throughout this period.

£400-600

◀ Made for a Scotland v England international in April 1907, the colours on the Scottish jersey were the racing colours of Lord Rosebery (primrose and rose hoops). This shirt and cap from the same match, belonged to Walter White. During his long career White played for Bolton Wanderers (1902-08), Everton (1908-10) and Fulham (1910-23), before retiring at 41. He represented Scotland twice against England.

£1,500-2,000

◀ This Ireland international No.5 jersey was worn by Con Martin, who represented the Republic of Ireland on 30 occasions, 1946-56., and Northern Ireland six times, 1947-50. Having opened his international career as Eire's substitute goalkeeper against Spain in 1946, Martin later played against England at centre-half, and was right-half in his debut for Northern Ireland.

£150-200

▲ Roy Vernon wore this red and white Wales international No.10 jersey in a qualifying match for the World Cup 1966 against Greece, on 17 March 1965. Vernon made 32 international appearances between 1957 and 1968.

£150-200

▲ The badge on this Manchester United shirt, showing a phoenix rising from the ashes, was used only once, in the 1958 FA Cup final, to symbolize the club's resurgence after the Munich air crash.

£800-1,200

▶ Made for the 1956-57 FA Cup final, this distinctive claret and blue shirt was worn by Stan Lynn of Aston Villa. Aston Villa defeated Manchester United 2-1 in the FA Cup final before a crowd of 100,000 at Wembley on Saturday 4 May 1957. Full-back Lynn scored 38 goals in 323 appearances for Aston Villa in his ten year service with the club.

£500-700

▲ Worn by Willie Waddell, the legendary Rangers and Scotland outside-right, this jersey was made for the Scotland-France international at Hampden Park, 16 May 1951. Waddell played in 17 Scottish internationals, and made over 550 appearances for Rangers, scoring 143 goals. He retired in 1956.

£300-500

▼ This jersey, which is typical of the style worn by England international footballers in the 1950s, was worn by Portsmouth's Jimmy Dickinson during the tour match against Italy, played on 18 May 1952, in Florence. Dickinson made a record 764 League appearances for Portsmouth between 1946 and 1965, played in 48 internationals between 1949 and 1957.

£300-500

Jerseys 2

In his *Handbook of Football*, published in 1867, Routledge suggests to the early reader of football literature how "one side with striped jerseys of one colour, say red; and the other with another, say blue" can help prevent confusion between two opposing football teams. It is certain that for the first FA Cup final in 1872, the two finalists, Wanderers and Royal Engineers, had adopted distinctive strips. Some clubs and national teams have remained faithful to the colours of their earliest shirts and kit, while others, like many clubs today, have changed their strip many times. In 1979, Scotland were the first international team to have the players' names inscribed on their shirts. Until the 1970s, the Football Association enforced strict rules and regulations governing the colours and patterns on shirts and strips. Goalkeepers were limited to green, scarlet, white and blue jerseys, while goalkeepers on international duty were restricted to yellow jerseys from 1921. Also, because of the huge number of football clubs that exist, every team has at least one set of change strip for use when their usual colours clash with those of their opponents – since 1924 visiting teams have to use their change strip when their usual colours are similar to those of their hosts.

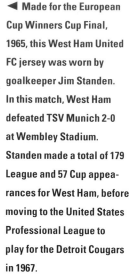

◀ Made for the European Cup Winners Cup Final, 1965, this West Ham United FC jersey was worn by goalkeeper Jim Standen. In this match, West Ham defeated TSV Munich 2-0 at Wembley Stadium. Standen made a total of 179 League and 57 Cup appearances for West Ham, before moving to the United States Professional League to play for the Detroit Cougars in 1967.

£400-600

▼ A collectable piece, this England No.9 international jersey, has been autographed by Bobby Charlton, c.1970. Charlton represented England in 9 internationals during 1970, and also made his last full International appearance against West Germany in the 1970 World Cup quarter-finals. During his career he scored a record 49 goals in 106 appearances for England.

£500-800

▲ A set of white jerseys including this No.8 example, probably worn by Katic, were made for Zurich, Switzerland for their European Cup match against Leeds United on 2 October 1974. Following a defeat in this game, Leeds went on to reach the final, before being beaten by Bayern Munich on 28 May 1975.

£80-120

▶ This Dutch shirt was worn by Ipswich Town's Arnold Muhren in a friendly between Scotland and Holland at Hampden Park on 23 March 1982. Muhren was born in Volendam, Holland. After winning a UEFA Cup winner's medal in 1980-81, he

joined Manchester United for the 1982-83 season and was a member of the 1983 FA Cup-winning side against Brighton & Hove Albion, scoring a penalty in the replay.

£80-120

▲ A jersey swap following a European Championship qualifying match in October 1978, gave this red Norwegian jersey to Scotland's Frank Gray. Scotland won this clash 3-2, but were beaten 4-0 in the next leg. Neither side went on to qualify, and the competition was eventually won by West Germany.

£80-120

▶ This Rangers shirt is believed to have been worn by Graeme Souness in the 5-1 defeat of Celtic in August 1988. Adding to the value of this piece are a number of autographs, including those of Chris Woods and Mark Walters. Rangers Football Club, founded in 1873, was one of the eleven founder members of the Scottish League when it was established in 1890.

£250-350

▲ Featuring the characteristic yellow and green of Brazil, this shirt is typical of those worn during the 1978 World Cup, held in Argentina. Brazil is the only country to have appeared in all ten World Cup tournaments, and the first to win the trophy outright.

£200-300

▼ A change strip in England's third-choice colour, this blue jersey was made to be worn by Gary Lineker in the 1986 World Cup in Mexico. In this tournament, England reached the quarter-finals where they were beaten 2-1 by Argentina, on 22 June 1986, in the Aztec Stadium before a crowd of 114,500. In this year Lineker received the Adidas Golden Boot award for being the competition's highest scoring player.

£300-500

Teams & Players

There is always a ripple of excitement amongst collectors of football memorabilia when "properties", as they are often referred to in auction catalogues or collections, relating to football players or club officials come on to the open market for sale. These collections, containing the awards and ephemera of the players, managers and officials of clubs that together make Association Football in Britain such a popular sport, have begun to come up for sale over the past 20 years or so, giving collectors the opportunity to purchase otherwise unobtainable examples of football memorabilia.

The metalware, kit and ephemera representing complete "careers" of some great players and important officials have already passed into the hands of collectors and enthusiasts, sometimes for surprisingly large sums of money. Their medals and awards, club/international shirts and caps, souvenir programmes and celebration menus, photographs and autographs and newspaper cuttings, and the other flotsam and jetsam that all types of people seem to collect unconsciously during their working lives, occasionally come onto the open market. The contents of these collections, be they ever so humble, are of supreme interest to any collector interested in football memorabilia.

To many collectors, the collections relating to players and officials represent the real stuff of collecting. It is easy to understand the attraction of such collections and the significance of owning and handling the awards and kit of great players and other football personalities of today and yesterday. This is an area where collecting can become very specialized. Some collectors may have very small collections, but what they have managed to collect may relate to just one player – perhaps their favourite player, or even their favourite player in his most memorable match. For example, imagine the pride in owning memorabilia of one of the "Class of '66" (the nickname of the celebrated England World Cup winning team): his 1966 World Cup winner's medal, and his red England 1966 World Cup final international shirt, the match ball and a match programme signed by the whole of the victorious team. Such precious items would probably realize around £20,000 if they were ever available for

collectors to purchase. However, regardless of their undoubted value, it would still be necessary for a member of that World Cup winning team to decide to offer them for sale.

Football is full of such collections. Admittedly not many feature World Cup winning medals, but there are a lot that include domestic league and competition medals, international caps and shirts, programmes, autographs and memorabilia from England, Scotland, Wales, Northern Ireland and Eire. Most never come up for sale, being kept by the players who won them, and after that by their families for many generations. Those that do come up for sale are eagerly sought after, especially as football memorabilia is still growing as a collecting interest. Notable players' collections that have have been offered for sale at auction recently include items belonging to Ray Kennedy (Arsenal, Liverpool and England), Frank Broome (Aston Villa, Derby County, Notts County and England), Dennis Viollet (Manchester United and England), Jim Standen (Luton Town, West Ham United and Detroit Cougars), Tommy Gemmell (Celtic and Scotland). These and other similar collections offer the most exciting source of memorabilia to collectors.

Left: A portrait of Ray Kennedy during the 1970-71 season while he was a member of the Arsenal double-winning team. *Background image:* Part of a collection of memorabilia amassed by George "Eddie" Edmonds. *Above:* A photographic postcard of Arthur Grimsdell, taken prior to his captaining Tottenham Hotspur to a 1-0 FA Cup victory over Wolverhampton Wanderers on 23 April 1923.

George Edmonds

George "Eddie" Edmonds, a big and bustling centre-forward, had a full and interesting football career and collected a handful of gold and silver medals to show for it. However, unlike many sportsmen he also kept many of the programmes, invitations, itineraries, postcards, photographs and printed ephemera that is of great interest to football historians and collectors. Born in 1893, George Edmonds shared much of his career with his life-long friend Arthur Grimsdell (see pp.130-31). They both played for Watford Fields schoolboy team before Edmonds joined Watford FC for the 1914-15 season and the team went on to win the Southern League Championship. In 1920 Edmonds joined Wolverhampton Wanderers where he remained until 1923. He joined Fulham and then returned to Watford for one last season in the summer of 1926. This collection attracted a great deal of attention when it came up for auction.

THE
FOOTBALL
ASSOCIATION

"VICTORY"
INTERNATIONAL
MATCH

ENGLAND v. WALES

To be played at "Ninian Park," Cardiff
on Saturday, October 11th, 1919
Kick-off 3 p.m.

▲ "Victory" internationals are classified as wartime matches. After the end of World War 1, eight international matches were organized to celebrate victory and peace. This programme is from the seventh, England v Wales, on 11 October 1919.

£80-120

◀ This 9ct gold Southern Football League Championship medal bears the inscription "G. Edmonds, Watford FC, 1919-20, Runners Up". George Edmonds had scored 20 of Watford's 69 goals during this season, before signing for Wolverhampton Wanderers, together, with team mate Val Gregory, for a reported fee of £3,000.

£150-300

▲ In 1924 Edmonds travelled with the England team as a reserve player for an England v France match on 17 May. The programme (top) is the itinerary that members of the team, reserves and members of the International Selection Committee received. Edmonds was notneeded as England defeated France 3-1. The card (bottom) is Edmonds' menu and programme of music from the post-match dinner and dance.

£80-120

► Edmond's FA Cup semi-final programme (right) from Wolverhampton Wanderers v Cardiff City, 19 March 1921, is in poor condition – not only has it been folded into quarters but its contents are also incomplete. The programme (far right) was produced for the Cup final, Spurs v Wolves, 23 April 1921. Once again Edmonds' copy is folded and stained. It is important to note that the value of these programmes lies mainly in their association with this well-known player.

£300-500 for the pair

▲ This postcard features a team portrait of the Wolverhampton Wanderers side that lost in the 1921 FA Cup final to Tottenham Hotspur. George Edmonds is described as "5ft 7½ in, 12st … the third London-born member of the team". It is creased in two places and its corners have lost their sharpness.

£30-40

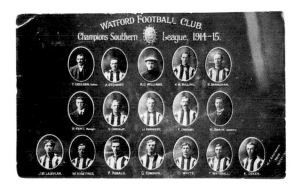

A programme from a Charity Shield match 1913, this game was one of only six to feature selected teams of amateurs and professionals.

£80-120

◄ A souvenir postcard celebrating Watford FC as Southern League Champions 1914-15; the previous season Watford Football Club had narrowly escaped relegation to Division 2 of that League.

£30-40

▼ The inscription on this 9ct gold Challenge Cup runners-up medal reads "G.W. Edmonds, Wolves v Spurs, April 23rd 1921". George Edmonds was very proud of this medal and is believed to have kept it with him at all times. It was the only match in which he played against his old school friend Arthur Grimsdell.

£400-600

Arthur Grimsdell

It is very interesting to compare the careers and collections of Arthur Grimsdell and George "Eddie" Edmonds: both played in the 1920-21 FA Cup Final and were at the peak of their careers during the 1920s. Best friends at school, they both joined Watford FC and played together until Grimsdell left to join Tottenham Hotspur in 1912.

Edmonds stayed with Watford until 1920-21, and then joined Division II Wolverhampton Wanderers. Tottenham's captain throughout the 1920s, Grimsdell made 324 League appearances for the club, scoring 24 goals, and was picked to represent England in six full internationals and two Victory internationals against Scotland. Grimsdell was Spurs' captain when they won the Cup in 1921. Afterwards he was photographed in an overcoat and hat outside Stamford bridge holding the Cup in one hand and some unopened post in the other. He then handed the Cup to the trainer and travelled home by train to Watford, not taking part in any of the celebrations. Collections such as these rarely come on to the market, but when they do they generate tremendous interest.

◄ The Victory internationals and Inter-League Victory matches played at the end of World War 1 did not count as full internationals, and medals were awarded to players rather than caps. This medal was awarded to Grimsdell who appeared in two such games in the 1918-19 season.

£200-300

► This 9ct gold FA Charity Shield medal was awarded to Arthur Grimsdell and, although neither inscribed or dated, it represents the game played by FA Cup winners Spurs against Burnley, the League Champions, in 1921. Although they are collectable, Charity Shield medals are not as popular as FA Cup or League medals.

£300-400

► Arthur Grimsdell represented England in six full international matches, 1920-23. Each was a Home International Championship game during a period when England was struggling to regain their pre-war form. This red England v Wales international cap was awarded to Grimsdell when England drew 2-2 in Cardiff, on 5 March 1923.

£300-400

► Grimsdell was presented with this 9ct gold medal when he was chosen to represent the Football League v the Scottish League at Hampden Park Glasgow, on 20 March 1920. These small oval medals are collectable, but the matches do not have the same status as internationals, hence the slightly lower price than would be asked for an equivalent international medal.

£200-300

▼ This pair of leather football boots produced during the 1920s belonged to Arthur Grimsdell. At this time football boots were largely handmade, with thick, inflexible leather soles and uppers, and became very heavy when they got wet. Old football boots are not rare or expensive, but it is unusual to discover a pair that actually belonged to a famous player.

£200-300

▲ Grimsdell captained Tottenham Hotspur to an FA Cup triumph against Wolves, who included his life-long friend Eddie Edmonds, at Stamford Bridge on 23 April 1921. In addition to his 15ct gold Cup winner's medal (see right), Grimsdell was awarded with this 9ct gold, cased pocket watch, inscribed and engraved with his monogram. The presentation case has been emblazoned in gilt with the club's ball and cockerel emblem.

£400-600

▼ During the 1920-21 season Spurs, in their first season back in Division 1, defeating Division 2 Wolves 1-0 in the FA Cup final. This collectable 15ct gold winner's medal was awarded to Grimsdell on 23 April 1921.

£1,500-2,000

► Tottenham Hotspur won the Division 2 Championship in the 1919-20 season, 6 points ahead of Huddersfield Town. This 9ct gold Football League Division 2 Champions medal was awarded to Grimsdell, then captain of the team. In this season Spurs won 32 matches and scored 102 goals. This medal is very collectable.

£400-600

Ray Kennedy

The Ray Kennedy Collection of football awards and memorabilia came up for sale by auction in October 1993. The lots, which spanned Kennedy's 17-year career, included medals, trophies, shirts and international caps. Collections such as this do not often appear on the market, especially during a player's lifetime, and attract a great deal of attention from serious collectors and fans alike.

Kennedy began his professional career with Arsenal in 1963, and enjoyed early success as part of the team's double-winning side in 1970-71. In July 1974, for the sum of £200,000 he became Bill Shankly's last signing and joined the phenomenally successful Liverpool side of the mid-1970s and early 1980s, scoring 72 goals in almost 400 appearances, and winning honours in the League, League Cup, UEFA Cup, European Cup and European Super Cup. He also played 17 international matches between 1976 and 1980. In 1982, Kennedy moved to Swansea City, winning two Welsh Cup medals, and then ended his playing career with Hartlepool in 1985.

▼ The Football League Cup began in 1960, but it was not until 1969-70 that all 92 clubs in the League participated for the first time. This gold and enamel medal, the reverse inscribed "Winners 1981" was presented to Kennedy when Liverpool defeated West Ham United 2-1 in the 1980-81 League Cup final replay on 1 April 1981, with goals from Kennedy and Kenny Dalglish. Kennedy appeared in all nine League Cup matches during this season, scoring two goals.

£2,000-3,000

▲ In the 1976-77 season Liverpool came within a whisker of bringing off an unprecedented treble of League Championship, FA Cup and European Cup. But Manchester United denied Liverpool their FA Cup win, beating them 2-1, and the Liverpool players each collected a runners-up medal.

£1,500-2,000

► While having played only two League matches for Arsenal during the 1969-70 season, Kennedy did make several appearances as substitute in the European Fairs Cup (now the UEFA Cup). He appeared as substitute in the first leg of the final against Anderlecht in Brussels. Following the second leg at Highbury, Arsenal won the competition 4-3. This replica miniature trophy (6¾ in, 17.1 cm) is inscribed with Kennedy's name, the title of the competition, and the date of the match.

£1,500-2,000

◀ This 9ct gold winner's medal and shirt are from the 1971 FA Cup final, won by Arsenal against Liverpool on 8 May. Arsenal had already beaten Spurs to win the League Championship on 3 May. The reverse of the medal is inscribed "The Football Association, Challenge Cup, Winners", and "Season 1970-71" appears on the rim. This yellow and blue No.10 jersey was worn by Ray Kennedy during the match. With this victory Arsenal achieved the double, becoming only the second side this century, and fourth in all to achieve this outstanding feat. Kennedy played 63 matches that season.

£3,000-5,000 medal £600-800 shirt

▼ Liverpool, Kennedy's new club, finished second in the championship in 1974-75, which won a place in the UEFA Cup in 1975-76. Reaching the final against Bruges, Liverpool won the first leg 3-2 including a goal by Kennedy, and a draw in the second leg gave the club the Cup. Kennedy made ten appearances and won this winner's medal.

£3,000-5,000

▲ In spite of their defeat in the FA Cup final, in 1977 Liverpool won the European Cup, beating Borussia, Moenchengladbach of Germany in Rome on 25 May. Ray Kennedy played in all nine of the European Cup matches in this season, scoring a goal against St Etienne, France, in the quarter-final. Each player received a gold winners' medal.

£7,000-9,000

▼ The European Super Cup is played between the winners of the European Cup and the winners of the European Cup Winners Cup. The 1977 Super Cup was played between Liverpool and SV Hamburg over two legs. The first was played in Hamburg and resulted in a 1-1 draw. The second at Anfield, ended in a 6-0 win for Liverpool. This medal is inscribed with the name and year of the competition.

£3,000-4,000

▲ In 1970-71 Arsenal became only the fourth club to achieve the League and FA Cup double, and Kennedy, who scored the goal which beat Spurs and settled the Championship, was presented with this League Championship plaque. The Gunners narrowly clinched the title for the first time in 18 years, with only one point more to spare over Leeds United.

£2,500-3,500

133

Manchester United 1

The autographed menus and programmes on these two pages came from "Jack" Pauline's unique and interesting collection of United ephemera. John Owen (Jack) Pauline was born in Liverpool but came to Manchester early in his career as an engineer with the Post Office and he joined Manchester United in 1944 to help with the junior teams. He stayed with the club for 34 years, working purely on a voluntary basis, during which he ran the "B" team and was involved in nurturing young talent. Nearly all the pre-Munich "Busby Babes" began their careers at United in Jack Pauline's "B" team – as did later talents such as George Best and Nobby Stiles. Jack retired in 1978 but remained a passionate United fan until his death in October, 1983. The rarity and desirability of these menus and programmes results from the familiarity of members of staff with players and management at any football club, circumstances not usually enjoyed by ordinary fans!

▲ This FA Cup programme and menu come from May 1957. In this year Manchester United were hoping to achieve a League and FA Cup double. The team suffered bad luck in the Cup final when goalkeeper Ray Wood was injured, and United eventually lost to Aston Villa by 2-1. The menu features autographs by Matt Busby, Bill Foulkes and Johnny Carey.

£300-400

▲ In March 1971 a dinner was held to commemorate 25 years of service to Manchester United FC by Sir Matt Busby CBE He became the club's manager in 1946 after a successful playing career with Manchester City and Liverpool. He later became director and then president of the club. Large and collectable, this menu bears a signed dedication from Busby.

£80-120

◄ In spite of the Munich air crash in 1958, Matt Busby's hastily rebuilt side succeeded in reaching the final of the FA Cup three months later. However, their opponents, Bolton Wanderers, denied them victory by winning 2-0 with both goals coming from Nat Lofthouse. This rare menu from the dinner and dance held at the Savoy in London to celebrate the match, includes 26 players' signatures and details of the after-dinner cabaret, which featured Max Bygraves, Harry Secombe, Norman Wisdom and Arthur Askey.

£200-300

▲ Shown here are two programmes and a ticket for the European Cup final between Benfica FC and Manchester United, held at Wembley, on 29 May 1968. United won 4-1, with goals from Charlton (2), Best and Kidd.

£1-5 ticket

£10-30 programme

£80-120 with autographs

▲ An autographed menu from the banquet at the Midland Hotel, Manchester, on 27 July 1968, to commemorate Manchester United winning the European Cup in the 1967-68 season.

£100-200

▲ In 1967 Manchester United became League Champions for the seventh time with 60 points from 24 wins and 12 draws. It was the club's fifth League Championship success since Matt Busby took over as manager in 1946. This menu from the celebratory dinner on 4 August, contains a number of autographs.

£80-120

◀ Manchester United won the League Championship in 1957, and this menu is from the celebratory dinner held in Manchester on 16 December. Matt Busby's "Babes" had won the League Championship convincingly with 64 points, having won 28 games and lost only 6, ahead of Tottenham Hotspur with 56 points. Tragically, less than two months after this dinner, on 6 February 1958, many of the team were killed in the Munich air disaster. This rare menu was autographed in ink by 27 Manchester United players and staff, including Matt Busby, Bill Foulkes and Bobby Charlton all survived the crash.

£300-400

Manchester United 2

With a collection such as this – specializing in one club during a certain period of time – it is not unreasonable to regard collectables and ephemera, such as programmes and autographs, as minor historical documents. Through these documents fans and collectors of football memorabilia can follow the development and success of teams, players and managers. In this case the team is Manchester United, one of England's greatest clubs, from 1956-57 to 1978-79; the players, in addition to the ill-fated "Busby Babes", included the considerable talents of many internationals such as Bobby Charlton, George Best, Dennis Law, Stuart Pearson, Lou Macari, Steve Coppell and Joe Jordan; while the list of managers since the war is headed by the great Sir Matt Busby and followed by Wilf McGuinness, Frank O'Farrell and Tommy Docherty. Collectors discover that all this – the successes and failures, the joys and sorrows – and much more, can be recalled in an immediate and very real sense through possessing associated souvenirs and memorabilia.

▼ In 1965-66, Manchester United was again England's representative in the European Cup. These programmes are from United's home-leg matches from the four rounds they competed in, against HJK Helsinki (Finland), ASK Vorwarts (East Berlin), Benfica (Portugal), and Partizan (Yugoslavia). Real Madrid won the competition for the sixth time.

£10-15 each

▲ A souvenir of the great soccer story of 1956-57, *The Red Devils* is an account of the "Busby Babes'" attempt at a treble, the League Championship, the FA Cup, and the European Cup. In the end they won the League, were runners-up in the FA Cup, and were semi-finalists in the European Cup. This example has been auto-graphed by many members of the team, and therefore, despite its untidy cover, is very collectable.

£200-300

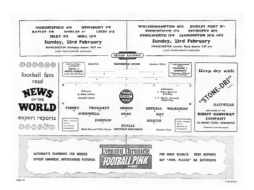

◄ This programme is interesting because it was produced for United's 5th round FA Cup tie against Sheffield Wednesday, on 19 February 1958, two weeks after the Munich disaster. No one was sure who would be representing United: blank spaces were left to be filled in on the day.

£20-60

▲ After losing the 1975-76 FA Cup Final to Southampton, Manchester United reached the final in 1977, this time facing Liverpool. A goal in the 55th minute gave United a 2-1 victory. Liverpool, however, went on to win the European Cup four days later. As with all FA Cup final programmes, this piece is collectable, but because it is a recent edition it is easily affordable.

£5-10

◄ Manchester United faced Real Madrid in the first leg of the semi-finals of the European Cup in April 1968 (left). They won 1-0 after a single goal by George Best. After a draw in the second leg (far left), they went on to become the first English team to win the Cup, beating Benfica 4-1.

£20-40 each

▼ These programmes are from the 1957-58 European Cup games when United met Eire's Shamrock Rovers.

£30-40 each

▲ This poster was presented with the *Manchester Evening News* following the Munich air crash on 6 February 1958. This small memorial poster is quite rare and, despite the poor condition of this example, is very collectable.

£20-30

Glossary

Cap Symbolic cap that is awarded to a player for an appearance in a national or representative side.

Centre-forward The player in the central position in the forward line, traditionally an accomplished goal-scorer.

Centre-half The player who occupies the central position of the defence. Latterly also known as a centre-back.

Charity Shield FA competition that was founded in 1908, currently played between the winners of the FA Premier League and the FA Cup.

European Championship formerly called the European Nations Cup, a UEFA competition for European nations held every four years.

European Cup/European Champion Clubs Cup Annual competition for Europe's Championship winning clubs, founded by UEFA in 1955.

European Cup Winners Cup The annual competition for Europe's Cup winning clubs, founded in 1961.

Extra time An extra period of play added at the end of a drawn knock-out match in order to produce a winner.

FA Cup The Football Association Challenge Cup was established in 1871, and is the oldest knock-out football competition in the world.

FIFA Formed in 1904, the Fédération Internationale de Football Associations is the body that rules on matters relating to international football.

The Football Association The governing authority of football in England, founded in 1863. The headquarters are based in London.

Football Association of Ireland The Republic of Ireland's FA was formed in June 1921. Based in Dublin.

The Football League Formed during March/April 1888, the leading professional League in England, before the formation of the FA Premier League in 1992.

Friendly A match that is not played as part of a competition.

Full-back A player in the last line of defence.

Half-back A midfield player who links the defence and the attack.

Hat-trick The scoring of three goals by a single player during a match.

Home International One of the international matches played between England, Scotland, Northern Ireland and Wales, in the British Home Championships. The competition was held until 1984.

Irish Football Association Based in Belfast, the Northern Irish FA was established on 18 November 1880.

Jules Rimet Trophy The name of the gold trophy awarded to the winners of the World Cup tournament between 1950 and 1970.

League Cup English Cup competition introduced in 1960, and restricted to members of the Football League and Premier League. Known as the Coca-Cola Cup since 1993.

Little Tin Idol Nickname of the original FA Cup.

Medals Commemorative medals and similar mementoes awarded to Championship winners and to players and officials who appear in football's major finals.

Penalty A direct free kick at goal from the penalty spot, first introduced by the Football League in 1891.

Premier League Formed in 1992 by the old Division 1 clubs breaking away from the Football League. Administered by the FA.

Programme Usually an official club publication sold at football matches containing details of players, the opposing team and other information.

Relegation The demotion of a football club from a division of a League to a lower one.

Scottish Football Association Based in Glasgow, the SFA was formed on 13 March 1873.

Spelter Zinc alloyed with lead used to produce inexpensive cast articles.

Tour A trip arranged to play a series of matches, usually friendlies and often overseas.

Transfer The deal that allows a player to move from one club to another.

UEFA The Union of European Football Associations, which is the governing body of European football, formed in 1954.

UEFA Cup Formerly the Inter-City Fairs Cup, a competition for leading European clubs who failed to qualify for the European Cup or Cup Winners Cup, founded in 1954.

Welsh Football Association First met on Wednesday 2 February 1876. Based in Cardiff.

Winger An attacking player positioned on the extreme flanks of the forward line.

World Cup Prestigious international football competition, held every four years, which was founded in 1930.

Useful Addresses

Association of Football
Badge Collectors
Keith Wilkinson
18 Hinton Street
Fairfield
Liverpool L6 3AR

Association of Football
Statisticians
22 Bretons
Basildon
Essex SS15 5BY

The Football Postcard
Collectors' Club
Brian Horsnell
275 Overdown Road
Tilehurst
Reading RG3 6NX

The Football Programme
Directory
David Stace
66 Southend Road
Wickford
Essex SS1 8EN

The National Football
Museum
Preston North End FC
Deepdale
Lancashire PR1 6RU

UK Programme
Collectors' Club
46 Milton Road
Kirkcaldy
Fife
Scotland KY1 1TL

Yore Publications
12 The Furrows
Harefield
Middlesex UB9 6AT

Auction Houses

Bonhams
Montpelier Galleries
Montpelier Street
Knightsbridge
London SW7 1HH
Contact:
Duncan Chilcott

Christie's Scotland
164-166 Bath Street
Glasgow
Scotland G2 4TG
Contact:
Grant MacDougall

Bibliography

Tony Ambrosen, *The
Illustrated Footballer*,
Breedon Books Sport,
1989
Gordon Andrews, *The
Datasport Book of Wartime
Football 1939-46*,
Datasport, 1989
Norman S. Barrett (Ed.),
*Purnell's Encyclopedia of
Association Football*,
Purnell & Sons, 1972
Bryon Butler, *The Football
League 1888-1988. The
Official Illustrated History*,
Macdonald Queen Anne
Press, 1987
Bryon Butler, *The Official
History of The Football
Association*, Macdonald
Queen Anne Press, 1991
Julian Earwaker, *The
Definitive Guide to Football
Programmes*, Chapter 6
Publishing, 1987
Maurice Golesworthy, *The
Encyclopaedia of Association
Football* 12th edition,
Robert Hale, 1976
Eric Krieger, *Good Old
Soccer – The Golden Age of
Football Picture Postcards*,
Longman, 1983
Norman Lovett,
*Football Programme
Collectors Handbook*, The
British Programme Club,
1974
Norman Lovett,
*Programmes and their
Prices*, The British
Programme Collectors
Club, 1977
*News of the World Football
Annual* – various editions
up to 1994, Invincible Press

David Pickering, *The
Cassell Soccer Companion*,
Cassell, 1994
*A Pictorial History of
Soccer Programmes*,
Volumes 1 and 2,
Matchday Programmes.
Jack Rollin, *The Guinness
Book of Soccer Facts & Feats*
editions 1-4, Guinness
Superlatives Ltd., 1978-
1981
*Rothmans Football
Yearbook* – various editions
up to 1994, Headline
Books
Phil Shaw, *Collecting
Football Programmes*,
Granada, 1980
Phil Shaw, *Whose game is it
anyway? The Book of the
Football Fanzines*, Argus
Books, 1989
Phil Soar, *The Hamlyn A-Z
of British Football Records*,
Hamlyn, 1981
Phil Soar, Martin Tyler &
Richard Widdows,
*Encyclopedia of World
Football*, Marshall
Cavendish, 1980
Martin Tyler & Phil Soar
(Ed.), *Encyclopedia of
British Football*, Collins,
1974
Martin Tyler, *The Story of
Football*, Marshall
Cavendish, 1976
Martin Tyler, *Cup Final
Extra! A Celebration for the
100th FA Cup Final. How
the Finals were Reported
1872-1980*, Hamlyn, 1981

Index

Acknowledgements

The publishers would like to thank the following auction houses,
museums, dealers, collectors and other sources for supplying pictures for use in this book
or for allowing their pieces to be photographed.

Key

b bottom, c centre, l left, r right, t top

10 tlB , main pic B; 11 GS; 12 all B; 13 all B; 14 all B; 15 all B; 16 all B; 17 all B; 18 all B; 19 all B; 20 all B; 21 all B; 22 all B; 23 all B; 24 all B; 25 all B; 26 all B; 27 all B; 28 all B; 29 all B; 30 all B; 31 all B; 32 all B; 33 all B; 34 all B; 35 all B; 36 all B; 37 all B; 38 all B; 39 all B; 40 all B; 41 all B; 42 clB, crCS, brB; 43 all B; 44 tlB, main pic DW; 45 B; 46 all B; 47 all B; 48 all B; 49 all B; 50 all B; 51 all B; 52 all B; 53 all B ; 54 all B; 55all B; 56 all B; 57 all B; 58 all B; 59 all B; 60 all B; 61 all B; 62 all B; 63 all B; 64 all B; 65 tlB, clB, blB, trB, crIPC; 66 tlGS, main pic B; 67 GS; 68 all B; 69 all B; 70 all B; 71 all B; 72 all B; 73 all B; 74 all B; 75 all B; 76 all GS; 77 all GS; 78 tB, clGS, crGS; 79 all GS; 80 all B; 81 all B; 82 all B; 83 all B; 84 all CS; 85 all CS; 86 all GS; 87 tlGS, blB, tcGS, cGS, brGS; 88 all GS; 89 all GS; 90 all B; 91 tlB, clB , blB, cB, trCS; 92 tlGS, clGS, bcB, crB; 93 tlCS, clGS, crPD, brGS; 94 all B; 95 clB, cB, bcB, trB, brGS; 96 all B; 97 all B; 98 clGS, blB, trCS; 99 tlCS, blGS, tcCS, cCS, crCS; 100 all CS; 101 clCS, blCS, trB, brGS; 102 all CS; 103 GS; 104 tGS, clCS, brB; 105 tlCS, clB, bB , trB, crCS; 106 tCSK, clCS, brGS; 107 tlCS, blGS, cB, bcGS, trCS; 108 tlCS, main pic B; 109 GS; 110 all CS; 111 tlCS, bcGS, crCS, trCS, brCS; 112 all CS; 113 all CS; 114 all CS; 115 tlGS, blCS, trCS, brCS; 116 all CS; 117 tlB, blCS, trCS, crCS, brCS; 118 tCS, bGS; 119 tlCS, clCS, blGS, cGS, trGS, brGS; 120 all GS; 121 tlCS, clCS, blCS, tCS, trGS, brGS; 122 all CS; 123 tlCS, clCS, cCS, trCS, brGS; 124 tlCS, blB, crCS; 125 tlCS, clCS, cGS, trCS, brGS; 126 tlCS, main pic B; 127 DW; 128 all B; 129 all B; 130 all DW; 131 all DW; 132 all CS; 133 all CS; 134 all B; 135 all B; 136 all B; 137 all B

B	Bonhams
CS	Christie's Scotland
CSK	Christie's South Kensington
DW	With the permission of Mrs Dorothy Woodward
GS	Graham Smith's collection photographed by Ian Booth for Reed Books
IPC	With the permission of IPC Magazines
PD	Paul Demby

The author would like to thank Alison Starling and Katie Piper for their boundless patience (well nearly) and hard work with this book. In addition, thanks are due to the following for their assistance and technical advice: Elizabeth Hand, Graham Smith, Grant MacDougall, Paul Demby and Mrs Dorothy Woodward.